Anxious Attachment Recovery

*Overcome Relationship Anxiety, Get Unstuck,
and Shift to Secure Attachment*

Susan Collins

Table of Content

Introduction

"Do you constantly feel anxious in your relationships?"

"Are you afraid that your partner might leave you at any moment?"

"Do you seek constant reassurance, but it never seems to be enough?"

"Do you find yourself obsessively checking your phone, waiting for a message?"

"Are your relationships an emotional rollercoaster, with moments of euphoria and deep despair?"

"Do you feel like you are 'too much' for others but can't control yourself?"

"Do you quickly get attached to people, only to feel overwhelmed by the fear of abandonment?"

"Do you interpret every little change as a sign that something is wrong?"

If these questions resonate deeply with you, you are not alone. Many of us struggle with anxious attachment, a condition that can turn love into an emotional minefield. But there is hope. The journey towards secure attachment begins here, with awareness and the willingness to change.

Maybe you recognize yourself in this daily struggle. Do you often find yourself staring at your phone screen, heart pounding as you wait for a response? An hour passes, then two, and your mind starts to race. "Maybe they're not interested in me anymore," you think. "What if they've met someone else?" Your fingers tremble as you type yet another message, asking if everything is okay.

Does this scene sound familiar? Do you feel trapped in a cycle of anxiety and doubt, unable to enjoy your relationships? Every moment of silence becomes torture, every ambiguous gesture a potential threat. You hate yourself for being so "needy," but you can't stop.

Or maybe you constantly find yourself sabotaging your relationships. As soon as things get serious, panic sets in. You convince yourself that your partner will leave you, so you start looking for every little flaw, every possible excuse to pull away. "It's better if I end it before they do," you tell yourself, ignoring the pain you feel every time a promising relationship crumbles in your hands.

This is the daily suffering of those who struggle with anxious attachment. The constant fear of abandonment, the incessant need for reassurance, the negative interpretation of every little signal: these are chains that prevent you from living authentic and fulfilling relationships. But it doesn't have to be this way.

Imagine waking up one morning and feeling a deep sense of calm within you. Your partner hasn't messaged you yet, but instead of panicking, you smile. You know they are fine and will reach out when they can. You get out of bed with a sense of security and confidence that permeates everything you do.

Visualize what your life could be like with secure attachment: Your relationships become sources of joy and support, not anxiety. You are able to express your needs without fear, and you calmly accept your partner's needs as well. Moments of separation are no longer reasons for distress but opportunities to cultivate your independence.

Imagine being able to fully enjoy moments of intimacy without the constant fear that they might end. Your self-esteem no longer depends on external reassurance but on a solid trust in yourself.

Think about how it would feel to handle conflicts constructively, without fearing that every argument could lead to abandonment. Your relationships become deeper and more authentic because you are able to show vulnerability without fear.

This is not an unattainable dream. It is the tangible result of a healing journey from anxious attachment. It is the freedom to love and be loved without the chains of fear. It is the promise of more fulfilling relationships, a deeper connection with yourself and others.

This book is your companion on this journey. It will guide you step by step towards this new reality, offering you the tools to transform your attachment style and, consequently, your life.

In this book, I will guide you through a transformative journey, providing you with practical tools and the knowledge needed to transition from anxious attachment to secure attachment. Here's what you will learn:

- Understand the roots of your anxious attachment by exploring past experiences that have shaped your way of relating to others.

- Learn to recognize your anxious thought and behavior patterns, the crucial first step in changing them.

- Acquire effective techniques to manage anxiety in relationships, such as mindfulness and emotional regulation.

- Develop strategies to communicate your needs and boundaries in a healthy way, without the fear of being abandoned.

- Discover how to build solid self-esteem, reducing dependence on external reassurance.

- Learn to handle conflicts constructively, avoiding the pitfalls of anxious attachment.

- I will show you how to cultivate more balanced and satisfying relationships based on mutual trust.

- Together, we will explore techniques to stay calm during moments of separation or uncertainty in the relationship.

- Learn to recognize and attract partners with a secure attachment style.

- Finally, I will provide you with a concrete action plan to consolidate these changes over time, gradually transforming your attachment style.

Each chapter will offer you not only theoretical information but also practical exercises, guided reflections, and concrete strategies that you can immediately apply in your daily life. Step by step, I will accompany you on this journey of personal growth, providing you with all the necessary tools to transform your relationships and your life.

My journey toward understanding and healing anxious attachment began with my own struggle. Growing up in a family environment marked by unstable relationships, I quickly developed an anxious attachment style that profoundly affected my adult life. For years, I lived my relationships in a state of constant insecurity, feeling the need for continual reassurance.

It was only after facing numerous relational challenges that I decided to take control of my life and address my attachment style. I embarked on an intense journey of research and practice, discovering the importance of developing a secure attachment style. I attended workshops, underwent therapy, and studied attachment psychology in depth. This journey led me to a deeper understanding of myself and relational dynamics, allowing me to live more authentically and harmoniously with others.

The transformation of my attachment style opened new horizons of creativity and allowed me to live in greater harmony with my true self. Having personally experienced the transformative benefits of living with greater inner peace and wisdom, I became passionate about sharing this growth opportunity with others.

This book is born from my personal experience, years of study and practice, and a desire to help those who, like I once did, feel trapped in the cycle of anxious attachment. I am not just an author theorizing about the subject; I am someone who has walked this path, who has personally experienced the pain of anxious attachment and the liberating joy of overcoming it.

My mission is to share the tools and techniques I have discovered and developed over the years, offering a practical guide for your personal journey toward healthier and more fulfilling relationships. This book is the culmination of all I have learned and lived, offered to you as a helping hand toward a more serene and satisfying relational life.

I continue to dedicate time to daily meditation and practice yoga, finding joy and serenity in my routines. Nature remains a constant source of inspiration and renewal for me, and I hope this book can be the beginning of an equally transformative and enriching journey for you.

This is not a self-diagnosis manual or a quick fix for relationship problems. It doesn't promise overnight miracles or offer a magical formula to instantly transform your attachment style. Instead, it is a practical and compassionate guide that will accompany you on a journey of self-discovery and growth.

Here you will find concrete tools, reflective exercises, and research-based strategies to understand and modify your attachment patterns. However, don't expect a clinical and detached approach. This book is not a substitute for professional therapy either. While it can be a powerful ally in your healing journey, in some cases, the support of a qualified therapist may be necessary. I encourage you to see this text as a complement, not an alternative, to professional support.

What you will find is an invitation to honestly examine your relational dynamics, challenge your limiting beliefs, and experiment with new ways of connecting with others and yourself. This journey requires courage, patience, and dedication, but it promises profound transformation.

As you progress through the book, you may discover parts of yourself you didn't know, face uncomfortable truths, and uncover unexpected potentials. This book is designed to be a trusted companion on this journey, offering support, encouragement, and practical guidance at every step.

Now that we've clarified what to expect, are you ready to embark on this journey of transformation? By turning the page, you will take the first step towards a new understanding of yourself and your relationships. I look forward to accompanying you on this adventure of growth and discovery.

With these words, I invite you to turn the page and begin your journey toward a more secure attachment. But before we dive into the first chapter, I'd like to share a final thought.

The change you are about to embark on is not just for you. By transforming your attachment style, you will create a positive ripple effect that extends far beyond your personal experience. Imagine how your relationships—with your partner, family, friends, and even colleagues—could flourish when you are anchored in a sense of inner security.

Every step you take towards secure attachment is a step towards a more connected and compassionate world. Your interactions will become more authentic, your relationships deeper, and your example will inspire those around you.

Remember, this is not a linear journey. There will be moments of challenge and doubt, but also moments of profound insight and joy. Embrace every part of this journey as an opportunity for growth.

As you prepare to turn this page, take a moment to breathe deeply. Acknowledge the courage it has taken to come this far and the commitment you are making to yourself.

The first chapter awaits, ready to guide you through the initial steps of this transformation. Are you ready to meet a more secure, more serene version of yourself? Then turn the page, and let's begin this extraordinary journey together.

Chapter 1:
How Does An Anxious Attachment Style Develop?

Have you ever wondered why some people seem constantly anxious in their relationships, while others navigate with apparent ease? The answer might lie in the earliest chapters of our personal history, in a part most of us don't consciously remember but profoundly shapes our way of loving and relating to others.

Anxious attachment, one of the four main attachment styles, is not an innate personality trait but rather a pattern of behavior and perception that develops in response to our earliest relationship experiences. These experiences, which occur primarily before the age of three, lay the foundation for how we will interpret and respond to relationships for the rest of our lives.

Imagine a newborn crying out of hunger or for comfort. In an ideal world, a parent or caregiver would promptly and consistently respond to these signals. But what happens when the response is unpredictable? Sometimes it comes quickly, other times it's delayed, and on some occasions, it might not come at all. It is in this ground of uncertainty that anxious attachment takes root.

The rapidly developing brain of the child, in its quest for patterns and predictability, starts to form a view of the world based on these inconsistent experiences. "Relationships are unpredictable," it seems to conclude. "I can never be sure my needs will be met." This conclusion, although painful, is actually an attempt by the brain to adapt and survive in a perceived uncertain environment.

But let's not stop here. The impact of these early experiences doesn't remain confined to childhood. Like a river carving its course, these attachment patterns continue to influence our adult relationships, often in ways we are not fully aware of. The adult with anxious attachment might find themselves constantly worried about abandonment, obsessively seeking reassurance, or trapped in a cycle of tumultuous relationships.

However, there is light at the end of the tunnel. Attachment styles, as deeply rooted as they may be, are not a life sentence. Our brain, with its extraordinary plasticity, retains the ability to change and adapt throughout life. With awareness, effort, and often with the help of professional support, it is possible to rewrite these attachment patterns.

In this chapter, we will explore in detail how anxious attachment develops, how it influences our adult relationships, and most importantly, how we can begin the journey toward a more secure attachment. Understanding our roots is the first step to cultivating a healthier and more fulfilling relational future.

The Impact of Inconsistent Early Experiences

Have you ever noticed how some children seem constantly in search of attention, while others appear more secure and independent? These differences are not random but often the result of profoundly different early experiences. In the case of anxious attachment, it is the inconsistency in early caregiving that plays a crucial role.

Let's imagine for a moment different family scenarios. In one case, we might have a parent struggling with alcohol or drug addiction. One day, this parent might be loving and attentive, the next day distant and inaccessible. In another scenario, we might find a well-intentioned parent overwhelmed by work or the care of multiple children, unable to provide consistent attention to the infant. Or we might have a parent facing mental or physical health challenges, wanting to be present but not always able to do so.

What do these seemingly different scenarios have in common? Unpredictability. The child never knows what to expect. Sometimes their needs are met promptly, other times they have to wait, and on some occasions, they might feel completely ignored. It's like living in a world where the rules of the game are constantly changing without notice.

This unpredictability profoundly impacts the child's developing worldview. The brain, desperately seeking patterns and predictability, begins to draw conclusions based on these inconsistent experiences. "Relationships are unstable," it seems to deduce. "I can never be sure that someone will be there for me when I need them."

But the child's brain does not simply draw passive conclusions. It actively seeks ways to adapt and survive in this uncertain environment. And this is where the amplification of emotional responses comes into play.

Imagine a baby crying out of hunger. The first time, perhaps, the parent responds promptly. The second time, the parent might be distracted, and the baby has to cry longer. The third time, the parent might be absent, and the baby has to cry even louder and longer to get attention. What does the baby learn from these experiences? That sometimes they need to "turn up the volume" of their emotions to get a response.

This emotional amplification becomes an adaptive strategy. The child learns that by showing exaggerated vulnerability or expressing intense anger, they are more likely to receive the attention and care they need. It's a strategy that works, at least in the short term, and thus it is reinforced and repeated.

But there is a price to pay for this strategy. The child never truly learns to regulate their own emotions independently. Instead, they become dependent on others' responses to feel calm and secure. This emotional dependence, born as a survival strategy in childhood, lays the groundwork for the anxious behavior patterns we see emerging in adult relationships.

Understanding these early dynamics is crucial not only for comprehending the origin of anxious attachment but also for beginning the healing journey. Recognizing that these strategies, however dysfunctional they may seem now, originated as intelligent attempts to adapt to an unpredictable environment is the first step toward self-compassion and change.

In the next section, we will explore how these early experiences translate into adult behavior patterns and how we can begin to rewrite these old strategies to create healthier and more fulfilling relationships.

The Role of Parents and Intergenerational Transmission

Attachment styles are silently passed down from generation to generation, creating an emotional legacy that is both powerful and invisible. This phenomenon is particularly evident in anxious attachment, where parents' relational patterns deeply shape their children's emotional experiences.

Consider the case of a parent who carries the scars of anxious attachment developed during their own childhood. This emotional background colors every interaction with their child, even when intentions are the best. Deep-seated beliefs about relationships—such as the idea that love is unpredictable, that abandonment is always looming, that emotions are unmanageable—seep into the countless nuances of daily life.

The transmission of these patterns occurs through a subtle interplay of reactions and behaviors. An anxious parent might react with excessive worry when the child ventures out to explore, unconsciously communicating that the world is a dangerous place. Or they might

16

feel overwhelmed by their own emotions in response to their child's anger or sadness, thereby depriving the child of an effective model for emotional regulation.

This process creates an emotional "blind spot": the emotions that the parent finds intolerable or incomprehensible in themselves become equally difficult to tolerate or understand in the child. Shame, for example, can become an emotional minefield. A parent struggling with this emotion might try to "fix" situations that evoke it in the child or withdraw emotionally, unable to offer the necessary support. The result? The child learns that certain emotions are too dangerous to express openly.

This mechanism repeats with various emotions—anger, sadness, fear—creating emotional "forbidden zones" that the child learns to avoid. But the impact goes further. Children, incredibly sensitive to their caregivers' emotional states, absorb their parents' anxiety, repressed anger, and unexpressed sadness. In the absence of explanations or models on how to manage these emotions, children often internalize them, taking on the responsibility of "fixing" or avoiding these emotional states in their parents.

Thus, a vicious cycle is established: the child develops hypersensitivity to others' emotional states, constantly modulating their own behavior to avoid negative reactions. This strategy, born as a survival mechanism in childhood, lays the groundwork for the relational anxiety that will characterize their adult relationships.

Understanding this dynamic of intergenerational transmission leads to a dual awareness. On one hand, it allows us to develop compassion for both ourselves and our parents, recognizing these patterns as learned behaviors rather than "faults." On the other hand, it provides a starting point for change, enabling us to identify and break these patterns, creating healthier models for ourselves and future generations.

This awareness naturally leads us to explore how these early learnings influence our ability to regulate emotions and how this manifests in our adult relationships. Emotional regulation is, in fact, the crucial bridge between our childhood experiences and our way of navigating the world of adult relationships.

Co-Regulation vs. Self-Regulation

The ability to manage one's emotions plays a crucial role in the development of our attachment patterns. This skill evolves over time, transitioning from total dependence on our caregivers to greater emotional autonomy.

In the early years of life, children rely almost exclusively on their parents or guardians to regulate their emotional states. This process, known as co-regulation, is essential for the child's emotional development. Through repeated and consistent interactions, the child should gradually acquire the tools to manage their own emotions independently, developing the capacity for self-regulation.

However, for those who develop anxious attachment, this crucial transition often does not occur optimally. As a result, these individuals, even as adults, continue to primarily rely on co-regulation in their relationships.

This dynamic manifests in various ways in adult relationships. People with anxious attachment tend to constantly seek emotional support from their partner, struggling to manage their emotions independently. They often believe that the only way to overcome a strong emotion is to share it with someone else and receive reassurance or comfort.

Consequently, these individuals may develop a view of romantic relationships as their primary source of emotional regulation. They may come to believe that a happy and committed romantic relationship is the solution to their emotional problems, providing a constant source of co-regulation.

However, this dependence on co-regulation can create difficulties in adult relationships. For a healthy and balanced relationship, both partners should be able to regulate their own emotions independently, choosing co-regulation when appropriate, but not relying exclusively on it.

The journey toward a more secure attachment for anxious individuals thus involves developing better self-regulation skills. This does not mean completely eliminating the need for emotional support from others, but rather finding a healthier balance between self-regulation and co-regulation in relationships.

Understanding and working on these mechanisms of emotional regulation can pave the way for profound and lasting changes in how we live and manage our interpersonal relationships.

Vulnerability and Anger

Anxious attachment often manifests through a characteristic oscillation between two seemingly opposite emotional states: extreme vulnerability and intense anger. These behavioral patterns, rooted in childhood experiences, play a significant role in the adult relationships of individuals with this attachment style.

In childhood, children who develop anxious attachment learn that certain emotional responses are more likely to attract the caregiver's attention. Specifically, displays of vulnerability or anger seem to be the most effective in eliciting a reaction. These strategies, born as attempts to obtain care and attention in an unpredictable environment, become an integral part of the child's emotional repertoire.

Vulnerability is expressed as an exaggeration of signals of need and dependence. The child may appear particularly helpless or in need of protection in an attempt to stimulate the caregiver's nurturing instinct. On the other hand, anger emerges as a response to frustration over unmet needs, a way to more forcefully and clearly communicate their necessities.

Over time, these behavioral patterns crystallize and are carried into adult relationships. People with anxious attachment can rapidly oscillate between states of extreme vulnerability and outbursts of anger, often in response to perceived threats to attachment or intimacy.

In moments of vulnerability, they may appear excessively needy for reassurance and comfort. They might constantly seek confirmation of their partner's love or express intense fears of abandonment. This vulnerability can also manifest through seductive behaviors or attempts to appear particularly desirable, hoping to secure the partner's attention and affection.

When vulnerability does not elicit the desired response, or when they perceive a threat to the relationship, they can quickly shift to anger. This anger can be expressed in various ways, from accusations of emotional neglect to attempts to control the partner's behavior. It's important to note that this anger, however intense, is often an expression of fear and insecurity rather than genuine hostility.

The impact of these behaviors on relational dynamics can be significant. The partner may feel overwhelmed by the constant demands for reassurance or confused by the rapid emotional shifts. This can lead to a cycle where the partner withdraws, provoking further anxiety and attachment behaviors in the anxious person.

Moreover, the oscillation between vulnerability and anger can create an atmosphere of unpredictability in the relationship. The partner may feel as if they are walking on eggshells, uncertain of which version of the person they will encounter at any given moment. This dynamic intriguingly mirrors the early attachment experiences, where the caregiver's unpredictable responses shaped the way the anxious person views and interacts with the relational world.

The Attraction to Avoidant Partners

People with anxious attachment often find themselves irresistibly drawn to partners with an avoidant attachment style. This dynamic, seemingly counterintuitive, has its roots in early attachment experiences and deeply shapes adult relationships.

The attraction to avoidant partners is not coincidental. Individuals with avoidant attachment tend not to openly display their negative emotions, appearing outwardly calm and in control. For the anxious person, accustomed to a tumultuous emotional world, this apparent stability is magnetic. Unconsciously, they see in the avoidant partner the secure and unflappable figure they have always longed for.

However, this perception is often an illusion. The avoidant partner is not necessarily better at managing emotions; rather, they tend to repress them. This emotional repression, mistaken for strength and stability, resonates with the anxious person's deep desire to find security and consistency in a relationship.

The dynamics that develop in these relationships are complex and often painful. The anxious person, constantly seeking reassurance and emotional connection, clashes with the avoidant partner's tendency to maintain emotional distance. This creates a cycle where the more the anxious person seeks closeness, the more the avoidant partner withdraws, further fueling anxiety and insecurity.

These dynamics strikingly reflect patterns learned in childhood. The anxious person, used to inconsistent care, finds the emotional distance of the avoidant partner familiar. Paradoxically, this familiarity, despite being painful, can be comforting, reproducing known relational patterns and thus, in a sense, predictable ones.

Expectations play a crucial role in these relationships. The anxious person hopes that, with enough love and dedication, they can "unlock" the repressed emotions of the avoidant partner. This hope, rarely realized, keeps the anxious person in a cycle of frustration and hope, always waiting for a change that may never come.

The impact of these relationships on emotional well-being can be significant. The continuous search for emotional connection, constantly frustrated, can lead to a deep sense of inadequacy and insecurity. The anxious person may find themselves trapped in a cycle of self-blame, believing that if only they were "enough," the partner would open up emotionally.

Yet, these relationships, despite their difficulties, also offer opportunities for growth and awareness. Through these experiences, the person with anxious attachment can begin to recognize their behavioral patterns and unrealistic expectations. This recognition can be the first step toward developing healthier and more fulfilling relationships.

The challenge for the anxious person becomes recognizing their intrinsic worth, independent of external validation. Learning to meet their own emotional needs, rather than constantly trying to fulfill them through another, can pave the way for more balanced and satisfying relationships.

Toward a New Horizon

In the chapters that follow, we will explore together the practical tools and psychological insights that will guide you on this journey. We will discover how to recognize attachment anxiety triggers, develop self-soothing strategies, and communicate more effectively in relationships.

Remember, this is not a journey you have to undertake alone. Alongside the resources you will find in this book, the support of a specialized therapist can be invaluable. And do not underestimate the power of healthy relationships in your life—understanding friends, family, or partners can be precious allies on your path.

Change is possible. With every page you turn, with every insight you gain, you will move closer to a version of yourself that is more secure, more serene, and more capable of loving and being loved fully.

Prepare yourself for an exciting journey. The road may seem long, but the destination—a life of more fulfilling relationships and a deeper sense of inner peace—is worth every step of the way.

Chapter 2:
10 Signs You May Have An Anxious Attachment Style

Have you ever felt a constant sense of uncertainty in your relationships, as if you were walking a tightrope in search of balance? This is the daily experience of someone with an anxious attachment style. Maybe you find yourself constantly seeking reassurance and validation, or you feel a deep fear of abandonment that you just can't shake off.

Identifying the signs of an anxious attachment style is crucial for better understanding yourself and the dynamics of your relationships. Recognizing these signs not only sheds light on behaviors and thoughts that might seem confusing or self-destructive but also represents the first step towards healing. Understanding that you have an anxious attachment style allows you to work on these dynamics, improving the quality of your relationships and developing greater emotional security.

In this chapter, we will explore ten distinctive signs of an anxious attachment style. These signs will provide a practical guide for recognizing and addressing behaviors that hinder a healthy and fulfilling relational life. Awareness is the first step towards change, and this chapter is dedicated to bringing to light the patterns that profoundly influence your relationships. Knowing these signs will give you the necessary tools to start a journey of personal growth and improvement, helping you build stronger and more satisfying relationships.

The Search for Feeling "Good Enough"

The first sign that you might have an anxious attachment style is the constant search to feel "good enough." Imagine waking up every morning with the feeling that you have to prove something, not just to others but to yourself as well. For those with an anxious attachment style, this is a daily reality. The relentless effort to feel "good enough" is like an endless marathon, with the finish line always moving a bit further away.

This incessant search profoundly impacts various aspects of daily life. At work, for example, it can manifest as extreme perfectionism. Every task, no matter how trivial, becomes a test to prove your competence and worth. Every mistake, no matter how minor, is perceived as confirmation of your inadequacy. This leads to a cycle of stress and self-criticism that can be extremely detrimental to mental health.

In social interactions, this dynamic translates into a constant quest for approval. Every word spoken, every gesture made, is calibrated to elicit a positive response from others. Self-evaluation heavily depends on others' opinions, making it difficult to develop a solid self-esteem. People with anxious attachment tend to surround themselves with those who can provide them with validation, but often this is not enough to quell their underlying insecurity.

Negative self-assessment is another central aspect of this search. Those with anxious attachment often view themselves through a distorted lens, emphasizing their flaws and minimizing their successes. Unrealistic expectations of themselves create a constant sense of failure. Even achievements are never enough to satisfy the internal need to feel adequate.

This continuous search to feel good enough can lead to emotional exhaustion. The fatigue of always having to prove something can be paralyzing. Mental and physical energies are constantly drained by this relentless effort, leaving little room for joy and spontaneity. Life becomes a series of tasks to complete rather than an experience to live.

A common example of this behavior is seen in romantic relationships. People with anxious attachment often find themselves doing everything to please their partner, even at the expense of their own needs. This can create an unbalanced dynamic, where their perceived value entirely depends on the partner's response. The fear of abandonment further fuels this search for validation, making it difficult to build a relationship based on trust and mutual balance.

Recognizing these behaviors and understanding their roots is the first step towards healing. It's important to start building a sense of self-esteem that is independent of others' opinions, working on your self-perception and learning to value your achievements, both big and small.

Being an Intimacy Junkie

Have you ever felt the urge to know everything about someone you just met, to go beyond small talk and dive deep into their thoughts and feelings? For those with an anxious attachment style, this desire can become almost compulsive. The intense need for intimacy drives these individuals to seek deep connections quickly, often pushing for levels of intimacy that their partners find too intense or premature.

This need for intimacy goes beyond a simple desire for emotional closeness. It's a real urgency, rooted in the fear of not being enough for the other person. People with anxious attachment try to fill this insecurity through a profound understanding of the other, hoping that an intense connection can offer them the reassurance they need.

The behavior of an intimacy junkie can be overwhelming for those on the receiving end. Imagine dating someone who, after just a few meetings, wants to know everything about your past, your fears, and your deepest dreams. This push to immediately explore the deeper levels of the relationship can seem excessive and make the partner feel pressured. Often, those subjected to this behavior may react by withdrawing, trying to reclaim their personal space.

The need to predict and control relationship dynamics is central to this behavior. Knowing everything about the other person allows for anticipating their reactions and temporarily alleviates the anxious individual's insecurity. However, this quest for control can be misinterpreted by the partner, who may feel smothered and invaded.

The combination of an anxious attachment style with an avoidant partner can be particularly challenging. The avoidant tends to withdraw in the face of emotional intensity, further triggering the anxious partner's need for reassurance. This creates a cycle of insecurity, where the anxious individual seeks even more intimacy and the avoidant partner distances themselves more and more.

In social situations, the person with anxious attachment may try to accelerate the process of getting to know someone, attempting to skip the initial phases of the relationship to get straight to the heart of the matter. This can be interpreted by others as an invasion of their personal space, creating a sense of discomfort and tension.

It's essential for those with an anxious attachment style to recognize this dynamic and work towards finding a balance. Calibrating the need for intimacy while respecting the partner's pace and boundaries is crucial for building healthy relationships. Developing a sense of security that doesn't solely depend on the immediate depth of connection with the other can help improve the quality of relationships and reduce the anxiety associated with attachment.

Disproportionate Commitment in Relationships

In relationships, it can sometimes feel like you're the one always putting in more effort, more emotion, and more love. For those with an anxious attachment style, this perception is almost constant. The feeling of being the only one truly investing in the relationship, of making more sacrifices, and of loving more is a common and often painful experience.

One of the main causes of this dynamic lies in partner choice. People with an anxious attachment style tend to be attracted to individuals with avoidant attachment styles. Avoidants are often perceived as independent and strong, qualities that can seem reassuring. However, their tendency to maintain emotional distance can exacerbate the anxiety and need for reassurance in the anxious partner.

This disproportionate emotional investment manifests in various ways. Someone with an anxious attachment style might do everything possible to maintain the relationship, often at the expense of their own needs and desires. This behavior can include daily acts of care and attention, personal sacrifices, and constantly adapting to the partner's needs. The goal is always the same: to avoid abandonment and ensure the other's affection and presence.

The consequences of this dynamic are often resentment and frustration. Constantly feeling like the only one making an effort can lead to a buildup of dissatisfaction and bitterness. The person with anxious attachment might start to feel unappreciated, exploited, or even mocked. This feeling, in turn, can further fuel their anxiety, creating a difficult cycle to break.

Moreover, this perception of disproportionate commitment can lead to controlling behaviors. The anxious individual might try to monitor and influence the partner's behavior in an attempt to gain more security and stability in the relationship. However, these behaviors can come across as oppressive to the partner, who may respond with further distancing and withdrawal.

A concrete example of this dynamic could be someone who, out of fear of losing their partner, constantly organizes activities, tries to make every moment special, and incessantly worries about the other's needs. If not balanced, this level of commitment can lead to an unbalanced relationship where the avoidant partner becomes accustomed to receiving without ever having to reciprocate the same level of attention and care.

Suppressing Your Own Needs to Please Others

At the beginning of a relationship, have you ever noticed yourself setting aside your desires and needs to avoid upsetting or scaring the other person? The fear of not being accepted for who you really are is one of the main psychological reasons behind this behavior. Instead of openly expressing their needs, people prefer to adapt to the expectations of their partner. This might provide a temporary sense of security, but in the long term, it creates a deep sense of dissatisfaction and frustration.

For example, you might agree to activities you don't enjoy just because you know your partner likes them. Or you might avoid expressing contrary opinions, fearing they might cause conflict or disagreement. This behavior not only hides your true personality but can also lead to a lopsided relationship where your needs are never considered.

When suppressed needs start to surface, conflicts inevitably arise. The mask you wore at the beginning of the relationship cannot be maintained forever. Over time, frustration grows, and your true desires and necessities emerge forcefully. This can confuse your partner, who has never seen this side of you, leading to tensions and misunderstandings.

Recognizing this pattern and starting to change your approach is essential. A useful strategy is to introspect and clearly identify your needs and desires. Write a list of things that are important to you in a relationship and evaluate if you are truly getting them. This will help you become more aware of what you are sacrificing.

Open communication with your partner is another crucial step. Instead of fearing rejection, try to express your needs clearly and assertively. It can be helpful to start with small steps, like choosing an activity you enjoy or expressing an opinion on a less sensitive topic. This not only strengthens your self-esteem but also helps your partner understand and respect your desires.

It's important to remember that a healthy relationship is based on a balance of mutual needs and desires. Constantly suppressing your needs will only fuel a cycle of dissatisfaction and resentment. Learning to balance giving and receiving in a relationship is crucial for the emotional well-being of both partners.

Being authentic and showing vulnerability may seem risky, but it is the only way to build a genuine and lasting connection. A relationship based on a false representation of yourself cannot withstand the challenges that inevitably arise. Being yourself, with your strengths and flaws, is key to building an authentic and fulfilling relationship.

Constant Worry About Relationships

Have you ever found yourself obsessing over every detail of a conversation with your partner, trying to decipher what that message or gesture really meant? For those with an anxious attachment style, this constant worry about relationships is a daily reality. This anxiety can take up a large part of your thoughts, making it difficult to focus on other aspects of life.

When you live with this incessant worry, every interaction becomes a detailed analysis. An unanswered message can trigger a flood of anxious thoughts: "Why haven't they replied? Have they lost interest? Is something wrong?" You find yourself scrutinizing every word and gesture, seeking reassurances that often don't come.

This worry isn't limited to conversations with your partner; it invades your interactions with friends and family as well. How many times have you talked to a friend just to seek validation for your relationship fears? This behavior can strain social relationships, as friends may feel overwhelmed by your constant need for emotional support.

The difference between healthy relationship concerns and obsessive worries is subtle but important. It's normal to worry about your relationship, especially when you care deeply. However, when these worries become pervasive and prevent you from enjoying other aspects of life, it enters the realm of obsession. You find yourself trapped in a cycle of anxiety and insecurity that seems impossible to break.

So, how can you better manage these anxieties? One effective strategy is to set specific times of the day to think about the relationship. For example, you might dedicate 15 minutes a day to reflect on these thoughts, preventing them from taking over every moment of your day.

Have you ever tried emotional "fact-checking"? When anxiety takes over, ask yourself: "What is my partner really saying to me? Is there concrete evidence for my fears, or are they just assumptions?" This helps you distinguish between reality and unfounded worries, bringing you back to a more balanced perspective.

Involving your partner in managing this anxiety can make a big difference. Talking openly about your fears and asking for reassurance in a clear and direct way can reduce uncertainty. It's important to do this in a manner that fosters open and sincere communication, without putting pressure on the other person.

Obsession with Your Partner's Thoughts and Feelings

Have you ever spent entire evenings wondering what your partner was thinking? Maybe a distant expression or a short message sent you spiraling into a whirlwind of doubts and fears. For those with an anxious attachment style, this obsession with their partner's thoughts and feelings is a daily reality. Every gesture, every word becomes a puzzle to solve, always with the worry that it might hide a sign of impending abandonment.

This hypervigilance has deep roots. Often, people with anxious attachment grew up in environments where affection and attention were intermittent and unpredictable. This led to the development of an emotional radar, constantly on alert to anticipate and prevent abandonment. Interpreting every slight change in the partner's behavior becomes a strategy to try to maintain emotional security.

Constantly analyzing your partner's behaviors can be exhausting. You find yourself mentally replaying every conversation, searching for hidden clues. If your partner is quieter than usual, your thoughts race: "What did I do wrong? Are they mad at me? Are they thinking of leaving me?" These thoughts create a cycle of anxiety that not only stresses you out but can also strain the relationship.

This obsession with your partner's thoughts and feelings often leads to dysfunctional behaviors. You might feel compelled to seek constant reassurance, repeatedly asking, "Do you still love me?" or "Are you sure you want to be with me?" This incessant need for confirmation can become a burden for your partner, who might feel smothered. Paradoxically, this can lead to further emotional distancing.

Another common behavior is constant monitoring of your partner. Checking social media, reading between the lines of messages, and scrutinizing every move with a critical eye are all manifestations of this obsession. If left unchecked, these behaviors can become invasive and undermine trust in the relationship.

To address this dynamic, it's important to work on self-awareness and recognizing your own fears. Learning to distinguish between perceptions and reality is crucial. Asking yourself, "Is there concrete evidence for my fears, or are they just assumptions?" can help reduce anxiety.

Fantasies and Loneliness

Have you ever felt loneliness become so overwhelming that you sought refuge in your fantasies? Maybe your partner was distant, or you were going through a particularly lonely period. For those with an anxious attachment style, retreating into imaginary worlds of ideal relationships is a common defense mechanism. When reality becomes too hard to bear, fantasies offer a safe haven where everything is perfect and the fears of abandonment vanish.

Often, people with anxious attachment create detailed scenarios in their minds, imagining ideal relationships where they are loved unconditionally. These imaginary worlds can become so enveloping that the line between fantasy and reality starts to blur. In your fantasies, your partner is always present, always attentive, always ready to provide security and affection. This starkly contrasts with reality, where uncertainty and insecurity are constant, making fantasies even more attractive.

However, constantly escaping into fantasies can have negative consequences. It can lead to a disconnection from reality. The more time you spend in your imaginary world, the less capable you become of facing the real challenges of your relationship. This can create a cycle of dissatisfaction, where reality always seems more disappointing compared to the perfection of your fantasies.

Have you ever avoided a conflict with your partner by retreating into your dreams? Fantasies can prevent you from addressing real issues in your relationship. Instead of confronting difficulties and working to improve the situation, you might find yourself avoiding conflict by escaping into your dreams. This not only fails to resolve problems but can make them worse over time, as unresolved issues tend to accumulate.

Another important aspect is that fantasies can create unrealistic expectations. When you constantly imagine a perfect partner, it becomes difficult to accept the imperfections and weaknesses of your real partner. This can lead to constant disappointment and frustration, as reality can never match up to your imaginary expectations.

To address these dynamics, try recognizing when you are using fantasies as a defense mechanism. Being aware of this behavior is the first step toward making changes. Reflect on what you truly desire and how you can work to achieve these things in reality, rather than in your fantasies.

Fantasies can offer temporary relief from loneliness, but it is by facing reality that true personal and relational growth is achieved. Even in the most intense moments of loneliness, trying to stay grounded in reality will allow you to tackle difficulties more constructively and create more authentic and fulfilling relationships.

Difficulty in Establishing and Maintaining Boundaries

The fear of pushing others away is rooted in the belief that your needs are not as valid as those of others. This leads to a constant willingness to compromise, even when it goes against your values or desires. For example, you might find yourself saying yes to requests you don't want to accept, just to avoid the risk of creating conflict or being perceived as selfish.

The lack of clear boundaries can lead to dysfunctional relational dynamics. Without boundaries, it's easy to feel exploited or disrespected, as others may not be aware of your limits. This can generate resentment and frustration, compromising the quality of the relationship and reducing your self-esteem. When you don't feel capable of protecting your boundaries, you begin to doubt your worth and your ability to command respect.

The consequences of a lack of boundaries also manifest in self-esteem. Every time you allow others to overstep your limits, you send a message to yourself that your needs are not important. This can lead to feelings of helplessness and insecurity, fueling a cycle of self-pity and low self-esteem.

To establish healthy boundaries, it is essential first to recognize and accept your needs. Take some time to reflect on what is truly important to you and what you are willing to tolerate in your relationships. Write down a list of your personal limits and values, and use it as a guide for making relational decisions.

Once you have identified your boundaries, communicating them clearly and assertively is the next step. Expressing your limits doesn't mean being aggressive or inflexible, but rather explaining respectfully what you need to feel safe and respected. For example, you could say, "I need some time for myself every day to recharge, so I would prefer not to receive calls after 9 PM."

Remember that setting boundaries is not a selfish act, but a necessity for maintaining healthy and balanced relationships. Your needs are as valid as those of others, and respecting them is essential for your emotional well-being.

It's also useful to prepare for possible negative reactions. Not everyone will understand or immediately accept your new limits, and some people might feel offended or rejected. This can be difficult to handle, especially if you fear conflict or disapproval. However, standing firm in your decisions and calmly explaining your reasons can help clarify things and enforce your boundaries.

Remember that you deserve to be respected and valued in your relationships. Recognizing and honoring your needs will help you build greater self-esteem and create more satisfying and respectful relationships.

Idealization and Disappointment

Have you ever met someone and immediately thought they were perfect? Perhaps in the early stages of the relationship, you found yourself idealizing your partner, attributing qualities to them that they may not fully possess. For those with an anxious attachment style, this tendency to idealize significant others is very common. You tend to see only the positive aspects, ignoring or minimizing the flaws.

However, this idealization often leads to great disappointment when the partner fails to meet unrealistic expectations.

At the beginning of a relationship, it's normal to be blinded by enthusiasm and infatuation. You see your partner through rose-colored glasses, imagining a perfect connection. Every kind gesture, every sweet word is amplified and interpreted as a sign of absolute compatibility. However, as time goes on, small imperfections and flaws begin to surface, and reality starts to set in.

When your partner fails to meet unrealistic expectations, the disappointment can be devastating. You find yourself wondering how you could have been so wrong. This leads to growing frustration and a continual search for confirmations that never come. Every little mistake or shortcoming is magnified, and the partner is judged harshly for not living up to your fantasies.

The causes of this behavior often lie in deep insecurities. Idealizing the partner is a way to seek security and stability. By seeing the other as perfect, you hope to build a relationship that can fill your fears and anxieties. However, this strategy is doomed to fail because no one can be perfect, and every relationship has its challenges.

To develop more realistic expectations, it's important to start seeing your partner as a complex human being with both strengths and weaknesses. A useful exercise might be to make a list of your partner's positive qualities along with their flaws. This helps you maintain a more balanced view and remember that everyone has both positive and negative aspects.

Worrying About Others' Opinions

Imagine receiving a compliment from a colleague. Instead of accepting it and feeling gratified, you find yourself seeking further confirmation, wondering if they really meant it or if it was said just to be polite. This constant need for external validation stems from deep-seated insecurity and the fear of not being enough. Every interaction becomes a sort of test, where the outcome is always uncertain and dependent on others' opinions.

This incessant search for approval can lead to self-destructive behaviors. You might find yourself saying or doing things just to please others, even if they go against your values or desires. This behavior not only compromises your authenticity but also leads to continual dissatisfaction and frustration. Every time you sacrifice a part of yourself to please others, you send a message to your self-esteem that your needs are not important.

Worrying about others' opinions often affects daily decisions as well. It can be difficult to make choices independently, without seeking approval or consensus from others. This can limit your ability to grow and develop as an individual, as your choices are guided by others' expectations rather than your own genuine desires.

To develop strong self-esteem independent of others' opinions, it is crucial to start recognizing and appreciating your intrinsic value. A useful exercise can be to write a list of your qualities and achievements, both big and small. Reading this list regularly can help you build a solid foundation of self-esteem, regardless of what others think.

It is important to practice self-reflection and self-awareness. Spend some time each day reflecting on your feelings and needs without judging yourself. Ask yourself: "What do I really want? What is important to me?" This will help you strengthen your sense of identity and make decisions that reflect your values.

Another crucial step is learning to say no. Refusing requests that do not align with your desires or that go against your values is an act of self-respect. Initially, it may be difficult, especially if you fear conflict or disapproval, but over time you will find that setting clear boundaries strengthens your self-esteem and allows you to live more authentically.

Finally, try to surround yourself with people who support and accept you for who you truly are. Positive and supportive relationships are essential for building and maintaining healthy self-esteem. These people will help remind you of your worth, regardless of others' opinions, and will encourage you to be yourself in every situation.

Chapter 3:
Why The Anxious Attachment Style Fears Intimacy

Imagine meeting someone who, after just a few encounters, wants to know everything about you—from your deepest dreams to your darkest traumas. You feel overwhelmed, perhaps a bit invaded, but this person seems genuinely eager to connect on a profound level. This dynamic, often observed in those with an anxious attachment style, is driven by an incessant need for emotional intensity. For these individuals, getting to know someone quickly and deeply is not just a desire but a necessity to feel secure in the relationship.

People with an anxious attachment style often express a fervent desire for emotional intimacy. They want to dive right into the heart of conversations, avoiding everyday trivialities. They feel an urgency to establish a deep and meaningful bond, almost as if each encounter is a unique opportunity to strengthen the connection. This quest for intensity can make these individuals seem like "intimacy junkies," always seeking a new "fix" of emotional closeness.

However, there is a crucial difference between getting to know someone quickly and developing true emotional intimacy. True intimacy requires time, boundaries, and mutual respect—elements often overlooked in the rush towards intensity. Getting to know someone rapidly might seem like a way to establish a deep connection, but it often leads to a merging of identities and a blurring of lines between what belongs to oneself and what belongs to the other. This phenomenon, known as enmeshment, is characterized by the fusion of individual identities, making it difficult to discern where one person ends and the other begins.

Enmeshment is not true intimacy. Authentic intimacy builds slowly, through the sharing of experiences, emotions, and thoughts, while maintaining clear boundaries that allow each individual to remain themselves. Without these boundaries, it is impossible to truly see the other person for who they are, as one is too entangled and confused to have a clear perspective. The ability to maintain and respect personal boundaries is fundamental to developing a healthy and lasting connection.

A practical example can help clarify this distinction. Imagine someone in a new relationship who systematically avoids small talk and immediately seeks to discuss past traumas, fears, and dreams. This approach might be perceived as an attempt to create a deep connection, but it often makes the other person uncomfortable, leading them to withdraw or feel overwhelmed. True intimacy, on the other hand, develops through a gradual mutual discovery, where both partners share and respect each other's pace and space.

The desire for emotional intensity often stems from a deep fear: the fear that, without an intense and immediate connection, the other person might drift away or lose interest. This fear drives people with anxious attachment to constantly seek reassurance and validation, trying to maintain the partner's attention and affection through a continuous emotional escalation. However, this strategy can backfire, leading to emotional exhaustion and frustration for both parties involved.

True emotional intimacy requires not only time and patience but also the ability to self-regulate emotionally. It means being able to tolerate uncertainty and distance without feeling threatened or abandoned. It's important to learn to appreciate the small moments of connection and to gradually build a bond based on mutual trust and respect for personal boundaries. Only through this slow and careful approach can a truly deep and meaningful connection develop.

Ultimately, the paradox of emotional intensity lies in the fact that, in the attempt to create an immediate and profound connection, one risks losing true intimacy. It is essential to recognize that intensity cannot replace the quality of the connection and that true intimacy requires time, clear boundaries, and a constant commitment to respecting and understanding the other in their uniqueness.

The Illusion of Intimacy and Enmeshment

Have you ever felt like you no longer know where you end and your partner begins? This state of confusion between self and other is what we call enmeshment. For those with an anxious attachment style, complete fusion with the partner may seem like the pinnacle of emotional connection. However, this fusion is not true intimacy, but a trap that hinders genuine connection.

People with an anxious attachment style often seek to eliminate the boundaries between themselves and their partner, hoping that this will lead to greater closeness. In reality, this lack of clear boundaries can lead to a host of problems. When two people lose their individuality within a relationship, it becomes difficult to see the other for who they really are. Every thought and feeling blends together, making it impossible to maintain a clear and objective perspective.

An example of enmeshment might be a couple in which one partner constantly needs reassurance while the other feels obliged to provide it, regardless of their own needs. This kind of dynamic leads to the continuous violation of personal boundaries, creating imbalance and resentment. In contrast, true intimacy develops when both partners can express their needs and desires without fear of losing the other.

Differentiation is the key to understanding and overcoming enmeshment. Differentiation means maintaining your own identity and autonomy while being in a close and loving relationship. It is the ability to remain yourself, with your own opinions, thoughts, and feelings, while sharing your life with another person. This ability allows each partner to grow and develop as an individual, while also contributing to the growth of the relationship.

Think of two trees growing next to each other. Their roots may intertwine underground, and their branches may touch in the wind, but each tree remains independent, with its own sturdy trunk and leaves. This is differentiation: two complete individuals who choose to share their lives together, rather than two halves that complete each other.

For those with an anxious attachment style, learning to differentiate can be challenging. Often, the fear of abandonment and the need for security drive them to seek fusion with the other. However, this fusion can stifle the relationship, leading to a lack of mutual respect and the loss of personal identity. True intimacy requires the courage to be oneself, to establish healthy boundaries, and to respect those of the partner.

A practical exercise to promote differentiation could be taking time for oneself, even within a relationship. This does not mean emotionally distancing oneself, but simply finding moments to cultivate personal interests, reflect on one's own thoughts and feelings, and maintain social relationships outside the couple. These moments of autonomy help strengthen individuality, making the relationship more balanced and healthy.

In summary, enmeshment is an illusion of intimacy that hinders genuine emotional connection. Differentiation, on the other hand, allows each partner to maintain their identity and build a relationship based on mutual respect and personal growth. Only by maintaining and respecting personal boundaries is it possible to develop true intimacy, in which both partners can truly see and understand each other.

The Limits of Intimacy

When Emily started her new relationship, she often felt overwhelmed by the need to be constantly available for her partner. Every time she tried to establish a boundary, she felt a growing anxiety, as if she were risking the relationship itself. This experience is common among many people with an anxious attachment style, who find boundaries threatening and difficult to maintain.

Personal boundaries are essential for healthy emotional intimacy, but for those with an anxious attachment style, they can seem like insurmountable barriers. The fear of abandonment and the constant need for reassurance drive these individuals to want to be always close, often at the expense of their own well-being and personal needs. However, it is precisely the absence of boundaries that can lead to toxic and unsatisfying relationship dynamics.

A practical example of how boundaries can improve a relationship can be seen when one partner decides to dedicate time to a personal hobby. Initially, this may cause anxiety in the other partner, who fears being neglected or abandoned. However, over time, the mutual respect for these personal spaces can strengthen the relationship, allowing both individuals to grow as people and as a couple.

Establishing and respecting boundaries requires communication and mutual understanding. It is important for both partners to openly discuss their needs and fears. For instance, Emily might explain to her partner how important it is for her to have some alone time to recharge, while her partner might express his concerns about this need for space. Through this communication, they can reach a compromise that satisfies both.

Another effective strategy is to set specific times when each partner can engage in their individual activities without feeling guilty or neglected. This not only allows them to maintain their identity within the relationship but also demonstrates respect and mutual trust. For example, dedicating one evening a week to individual activities can help maintain a healthy balance between the couple's life and personal needs.

The fear of setting boundaries is often rooted in past experiences where the need for space was perceived as a sign of rejection or abandonment. Overcoming this fear requires significant inner work, which may include personal reflection and, in some cases, the support of a therapist. Recognizing that boundaries are not barriers but tools for protection and personal growth is a crucial step for anyone wishing to build healthier and more fulfilling relationships.

An illuminating example can be drawn from the experience of John, who learned to set boundaries after years of unsatisfying relationships. John recounts how he began dedicating time to daily meditation, explaining to his partner how important this was for his emotional balance. Despite initial resistance, his partner learned to respect this space, also noticing an improvement in the quality of the time they spent together.

Finally, it is essential to remember that boundaries are not static but can evolve with the growth of the relationship and the people involved. It is important to be flexible and open to renegotiating boundaries as needs and circumstances change. The key is to maintain open and honest communication, where both partners feel free to express their needs without fear of judgment or rejection.

Personal boundaries should not be seen as obstacles to intimacy but rather as the foundations upon which to build a healthy and lasting relationship. Learning to establish and respect them can radically transform the quality of our relationships, allowing us to experience more authentic and fulfilling connections.

The Role of Savior Fantasies

Have you ever dreamed of finding a partner who could solve all your emotional problems, someone who understands every need without you having to explain anything? This type of fantasy is common among people with an anxious attachment style. It's a romantic and idealized notion of a savior partner who arrives to heal all past wounds and provide complete emotional security.

These savior fantasies often begin in childhood, when experiences of care and affection were intermittent or insufficient. The idea that someone will come along one day to fill all the gaps can become a mental refuge, a hope that offers temporary relief from pain and insecurity. However, when these fantasies are projected into adult relationships, they can lead to a series of problems.

Take Emily, for example, who spent much of her life waiting for her "knight in shining armor." Every time she started a new relationship, she immediately invested all her hopes in this person, convincing herself that she had finally found someone who would solve all her emotional problems. However, over time, she realized that no one could bear the weight of these unrealistic expectations, leading to constant disappointment and frustration.

These fantasies also influence partner choice. People with anxious attachment are often drawn to avoidant individuals. The latter, who tend to maintain emotional distance, can initially appear stable and secure—exactly what the anxious person is seeking. However, this combination is often dysfunctional. The anxious person constantly seeks reassurance and closeness, while the avoidant partner withdraws to protect their space, creating a cycle of insecurity and conflict.

The implications of these savior fantasies on personal growth are significant. When a person is constantly looking for an external savior, they lose sight of the importance of emotional self-sufficiency. Instead of developing internal tools to manage their own emotions and needs, they delegate this responsibility to their partner, risking their own growth and well-being.

Consider John, a man with an anxious attachment style, who moved from one relationship to another, desperately seeking someone who could finally understand and accept him completely. However, as soon as the first signs of conflict or distance emerged, his insecurity exploded, making it impossible to maintain a stable relationship. It was only when John began to work on himself, developing greater emotional self-sufficiency, that he was able to build a more balanced and satisfying relationship.

For anyone who recognizes these dynamics, it is crucial to start cultivating emotional self-sufficiency. This doesn't mean closing oneself off to love or relationships, but rather developing a solid sense of self that doesn't entirely depend on a partner's approval or proximity. Learning to manage one's emotions, find comfort within oneself, and build a diversified support network can make a significant difference.

A practical exercise might be to identify your unrealistic expectations of your partner and reflect on how these influence the relationship. Ask yourself: "Am I placing all my insecurities and emotional needs on my partner? What can I do to cultivate my emotional self-sufficiency?" Writing down these reflections and discussing them with a therapist or a trusted friend can help focus on these aspects and work through them.

Savior fantasies, while enticing, can hinder true intimacy and significant personal growth. Recognizing and working on these dynamics is essential to building healthier and more fulfilling relationships, based not on the need to be saved, but on the ability to support each other as complete and autonomous individuals.

Avoiding Personal Vulnerabilities

Imagine being in a relationship where you constantly feel pressured to appear perfect, never showing your weaknesses. This is often the case for people with an anxious attachment style, who struggle to recognize and accept their imperfections and vulnerabilities. The fear of being judged or rejected pushes them to present an idealized version of themselves, hiding aspects they consider unacceptable.

True emotional intimacy requires the ability to be authentic, to accept both your strengths and weaknesses. However, for those with an anxious attachment style, showing their vulnerabilities can seem like too great a risk. They fear that revealing their most fragile sides could lead to losing their partner's love and acceptance. This avoidance of vulnerabilities becomes a significant barrier to genuine emotional connection.

How would your relationship change if you could show your weaknesses without fear of being judged? Reflecting on this question can help you understand the importance of sharing your vulnerabilities to build a deeper and more authentic connection.

To overcome this fear, it's necessary to start with small steps. A useful strategy might be to gradually share small vulnerabilities with your partner. Think about which small aspects of your life you can start to share that you have never revealed before. Begin talking about these experiences and see how your relationship begins to transform.

Accepting your imperfections is an ongoing challenge for those with an anxious attachment style. One helpful exercise could be to practice self-compassion. Instead of harshly judging yourself for your weaknesses, it's important to learn to treat yourself with the same kindness and understanding you would offer a friend. This approach can help reduce the anxiety linked to exposing vulnerabilities and promote greater self-acceptance.

Consider the importance of talking about your fears and insecurities in a safe and non-judgmental environment. How would your life change if you could openly express your feelings without fear of being judged?

Assertive communication is another valuable tool. Are you able to express your needs and feelings clearly and respectfully? Learning to say "I feel insecure when..." or "I need support with this..." can help create open and honest dialogue, strengthening the emotional connection with your partner.

Avoiding personal vulnerabilities prevents true emotional intimacy. Addressing and overcoming this fear requires time, patience, and practice, but the benefits that result can radically transform the quality of relationships, allowing for a more authentic and fulfilling connection.

Healing and Personal Growth

Have you ever wondered what it would be like to feel truly secure and stable in your relationships, without depending on constant reassurance from others? For people with an anxious attachment style, developing a secure base within themselves is a crucial but achievable challenge. This section will explore various strategies to improve emotional self-regulation and build greater emotional security.

One of the most effective techniques for developing a secure base is mindfulness. Practicing mindfulness helps you become more aware of your thoughts and emotions in the present moment, without judgment. You can start with simple breathing exercises: sit in a quiet place, close your eyes, and focus on your breath. Notice how it enters and exits your lungs, and when your mind starts to wander, gently bring it back to your breath. This exercise can help reduce anxiety and improve your ability to stay calm in stressful situations.

Another useful technique is cognitive-behavioral therapy (CBT). CBT focuses on changing negative thoughts and dysfunctional behaviors that contribute to anxiety and insecurity. For example, if you tend to think, "My partner will leave me if I don't respond to their messages immediately," CBT helps you recognize this thought as irrational and replace it with a more realistic and positive one, such as, "My partner loves me, and I don't need to respond immediately to maintain their affection." Working with a therapist can provide practical tools to manage these thoughts and improve your self-esteem.

Building a sense of self-esteem independent of external validation is essential. How can you start valuing yourself for who you are, rather than for what others think of you? A practical exercise is to write down three things you are proud of or grateful for each day. This can help you develop a more positive view of yourself and recognize your intrinsic worth.

Imagine how your life would change if you could rely on your inner strength rather than constantly seeking approval from others. Ask yourself: "What are the qualities I most appreciate in myself? How can I cultivate them further?" Reflecting on these questions will help you focus on what is truly important for your emotional well-being.

Establishing more balanced and satisfying relationships also requires the ability to set and respect your boundaries. Are you able to say "no" when necessary? How do you feel when you have to assert your needs? Practicing assertiveness by clearly and respectfully expressing your desires and limits can significantly improve the quality of your relationships. You can start with small steps, such as deciding to take time for yourself without feeling guilty.

A useful exercise to develop assertiveness is to write a list of your needs and desires, and then practice expressing them out loud, first to yourself and then to a trusted person. This will help you become more confident in communicating your needs to others.

Healing and personal growth require time and dedication, but with consistent practices like mindfulness and CBT, and focusing on developing healthy self-esteem and assertiveness, it is possible to build an emotionally stable life and more fulfilling relationships.

Chapter 4:
Understanding Triggers

Imagine walking down the street peacefully when suddenly, a sharp sound makes you jump. Your heart races, your palms sweat, and for a moment, you feel catapulted to another place, another time. This is a trigger in action. But what does it really mean to be "triggered"? And how has this concept evolved in everyday language?

The term "trigger" has deep roots in clinical psychology, where it originally referred to stimuli that provoked intense reactions in individuals with Post-Traumatic Stress Disorder (PTSD) or Complex Post-Traumatic Stress Disorder (C-PTSD). In these contexts, a trigger can cause an overwhelming emotional and physical response, bringing the person back to relive a past trauma with unsettling vividness.

However, over time, the use of the term has expanded well beyond clinical boundaries. In today's popular culture, "being triggered" can refer to a wide range of emotional reactions, from mild annoyance to strong indignation. This linguistic evolution has led to a kind of trivialization of the concept, often creating confusion between serious traumatic reactions and simple moments of emotional discomfort.

It's crucial to recognize this distinction. While a clinical trigger can completely paralyze a person, rendering them unable to function normally, a trigger in the broader sense of the term might simply intensify an emotional reaction, while still leaving the individual able to manage the situation, albeit with difficulty.

This new understanding of triggers invites us to greater awareness of our emotional reactions. It's not about minimizing our experiences, but rather calibrating our response appropriately. Recognizing that we are "triggered" doesn't necessarily mean we're victims of deep trauma, but it may indicate that we're reacting to a present situation through the filter of past experiences.

The challenge, then, lies in navigating this spectrum of reactions with wisdom and compassion. How can we distinguish between a trigger that requires professional intervention and one we can manage with mindfulness techniques? How can we honor the gravity of clinical triggers without ignoring the real impact that less intense reactions can have on our daily lives?

Awareness is the first step. Observing our reactions, noticing patterns that repeat, and trying to understand where these emotional responses come from are all crucial elements in our journey of personal growth. This process of self-observation allows us not only to better manage our triggers but also to develop greater empathy towards others and their reactions.

Remember, it's not about judging our emotional responses as "right" or "wrong". Every reaction, whether it's a clinical trigger or an intensified emotional response, deserves respect and attention. The goal is to develop tools to navigate these emotional waters with grace and resilience, recognizing when we need professional help and when we can rely on our internal resources.

Throughout this chapter, we'll explore various aspects of this complex emotional landscape. We'll learn to recognize our body's signals, separate past reactions from present situations, and develop strategies to respond more consciously to our triggers. This journey of self-discovery doesn't promise to completely eliminate triggers from our lives, but it offers us the possibility of transforming them into opportunities for growth and deeper self-understanding.

The Fine Line Between Trigger and Truth

Have you ever found yourself in a situation where you were certain you were right, but at the same time felt a wave of overwhelming emotions threatening to engulf you? Welcome to the complex territory where triggers intertwine with objective reality.

Many of us fall into the trap of black-and-white thinking when it comes to emotional reactions. On one hand, we might think, "I'm completely wrong, the other person is right, and my reaction is pure trigger." On the other, we might convince ourselves, "I'm absolutely right, I'm 100% justified in feeling offended, and therefore anything I say or do is completely justified." This false dichotomy is at the root of many unresolved conflicts and missed opportunities for personal growth.

The truth is that often the situations that trigger us are precisely those where a real injustice is occurring. The trick is recognizing that both things can be true simultaneously: you can be right about the substance of the issue and at the same time be triggered disproportionately to the current situation.

Imagine you're in a work meeting and a colleague makes a dismissive comment about your project. Your heart starts beating faster, you feel heat rising to your face, and suddenly you're flooded with memories of all the times you've felt belittled or unappreciated. In this moment, you're experiencing both a real injustice (the colleague's inappropriate comment) and a triggered reaction (the intensity of your emotional response fueled by past experiences).

The danger lies in letting the triggered reaction obscure the legitimacy of your concerns. When we respond from a heightened emotional state, we risk overreacting, losing sight of the main point, or behaving in ways that allow others to dismiss our concerns as irrational or excessive.

The key to navigating this treacherous terrain is developing the ability to recognize both aspects of the situation. Start by asking yourself, "What about what's happening right now is making me react? And how much of my reaction is coming from past experiences or future fears?"

This process of discernment requires practice and patience. It's not about suppressing your emotions or denying the validity of your feelings. On the contrary, it's about creating a space between stimulus and response, a moment of awareness where you can recognize both the objective reality of the situation and the intensity of your emotional reaction.

A useful exercise is keeping a "trigger diary." Every time you feel yourself reacting strongly to a situation, take a moment to write down what objectively happened and how you felt. Over time, you might start noticing patterns in your reactions, helping you more easily distinguish between triggers and genuine concerns of the present moment.

Remember, the goal isn't to eliminate your emotional reactions, but rather to learn to respond in a more balanced and effective way. Recognizing that you can be both triggered and in the right allows you to approach situations with greater clarity and compassion, both towards yourself and others.

As we progress on our journey of self-discovery, it's crucial to maintain an open and curious mind. Every trigger, every intense reaction, is an opportunity to learn something new about ourselves and how we interact with the world around us. With practice and persistence, we can learn to navigate the delicate balance between being triggered and being right, transforming potential conflicts into opportunities for growth and mutual understanding.

Recognizing Body Signals: The Physical Awareness of Triggers

Your body is a silent storyteller, narrating tales that your rational mind might not immediately grasp. When it comes to emotional triggers, your body often knows before you're consciously aware. But how can we tune into these subtle signals and use them as tools for greater emotional awareness?

Imagine walking into a crowded room. Before you consciously process the situation, you might notice your breath becoming shallower, your shoulders tensing, or a knot forming in your stomach. These are examples of how your body reacts to a potential trigger before your rational mind has time to analyze the situation.

Everyone has their own unique physical "signature" when it comes to triggers. For some, it might manifest as a sudden flush of heat to the face, for others, it could be a tingling in the hands or tension in the jaw. The first step in developing greater trigger awareness is learning to recognize these specific bodily signals.

A useful exercise is to practice "body scanning" regularly, especially in situations you know to be potentially triggering. Close your eyes and bring your attention slowly from head to toe, noticing every sensation along the way. With practice, you'll become more skilled at recognizing the subtle changes in your physical state that signal the onset of a triggered reaction.

It's important to remember that these physical reactions are neither good nor bad; they're simply information. Your body is trying to communicate something important about your emotional experience. Welcoming these sensations with curiosity rather than judgment is key to developing a more harmonious relationship with your triggers.

Once you've learned to recognize your bodily signals, you can start using them as an early warning system. When you notice the physical signs of a trigger activating, you have the opportunity to mentally step back and assess the situation more objectively. This moment of pause can make the difference between an impulsive reaction and a thoughtful response.

Consider, for example, a situation where you feel criticized during a work meeting. Before fully processing the words spoken, you might notice your heart starting to beat faster and your fists clenching. By recognizing these signals, you can take a deep breath and ask yourself, "What's really happening here? Is my reaction proportionate to the current situation, or am I bringing past experiences into this?"

Physical awareness of triggers not only helps you better manage your reactions in the moment but can also provide valuable insights into deeper emotional patterns. Over time, you might notice that certain types of situations or interactions consistently provoke the same physical responses. This awareness can be the starting point for exploring and healing long-standing emotional wounds.

Integrating this bodily awareness into your daily life requires practice and patience. You might find it helpful to keep a journal of your experiences, noting not just the triggering events but also the associated physical sensations. This can help you map your internal emotional landscape and develop personalized strategies for navigating it with greater grace.

Remember, the goal isn't to completely eliminate triggered reactions - these are a natural part of our human experience. Rather, we're seeking to develop a more conscious and compassionate relationship with our emotional responses. By listening closely to your body's signals, you're laying the groundwork for greater emotional resilience and a deeper understanding of yourself.

Strategies for Separating Past from Present

Imagine having an emotional time machine, capable of instantly transporting you from the here and now to moments in your past. This is essentially what happens when we're triggered: in the blink of an eye, we find ourselves reliving emotions and reactions that belong to past experiences, often without realizing we're reacting more to our history than to the current situation.

The first step in breaking this cycle is developing the ability to distinguish between what's actually happening in the present and what we're bringing from our past. This process begins with a simple question: "What, exactly, in the last five minutes, made me react so intensely?"

This question forces us to focus on concrete and immediate facts, separating them from the broader emotional narrative we might be constructing in our minds. Often, when we closely examine the present situation, we discover that our reaction is disproportionate to the actual triggering event.

A useful exercise is practicing "objective description." When you feel triggered, try to describe the situation as if you were a security camera, focusing only on what can be objectively seen or heard. This helps separate facts from the interpretations and emotions we attach to them.

Another powerful tool is the practice of "emotional time travel." When you notice you're triggered, try asking yourself: "How old am I right now?" Often, you'll find that emotionally you feel much younger than your current age. This can be a clear sign that you're reacting from a more vulnerable and younger part of yourself, rather than from your adult, present self.

Recognizing this "emotional regression" can be illuminating. It allows you to see how your past experiences are influencing your perception of the present. Once you've identified this pattern, you can begin to "re-parent" yourself, offering your younger, more vulnerable part the support and understanding it needed in the past.

Another effective approach is creating an "evidence journal." Whenever you feel triggered, note down not only the triggering event but also the "evidence" supporting your emotional reaction. Then, challenge yourself to find contrary evidence. This exercise can help you see how your interpretations may be influenced by past experiences rather than present reality.

It's important to remember that the goal isn't to deny or suppress your emotions, but rather to develop a more conscious relationship with them. Your emotional reactions, even when they seem disproportionate, contain valuable information about your personal history and unmet needs.

By practicing these techniques regularly, you'll start to notice greater fluidity in how you navigate between past and present. You'll become more skilled at recognizing when you're projecting past experiences onto the current situation and be able to respond more appropriately to the here and now.

This process of separating past from present not only helps you better manage triggers, but also opens the door to deeper healing. By recognizing and honoring the parts of you that still carry the weight of past experiences, you create space for true transformation and emotional growth.

Trigger Management Techniques

Have you ever felt like a pressure cooker about to explode? This is often what we experience when we're strongly triggered. The urge to react immediately can be overwhelming, but it's precisely in these moments that a measured, mindful response can make all the difference.

The first step towards effective trigger management is recognizing that you always have a choice. Even if it feels like your reaction is automatic and inevitable, there's always a microscopic space between stimulus and response. This space, however small, is your point of power.

A powerful technique to expand this space is the practice of the "emergency breath." When you feel overwhelmed by a trigger, take a deep breath, slowly counting to four as you inhale and to six as you exhale. This simple act not only oxygenates the brain, helping you think more clearly, but also creates a crucial moment of pause between the triggering event and your reaction.

Another useful tool is the "naming technique." When you feel the wave of emotions rising, try to name the feeling you're experiencing. "This is anger," "This is fear," "This is shame." The act of labeling your emotions can help you distance yourself slightly from them, offering a more objective perspective.

The practice of the "future self" can be particularly effective. Imagine being able to talk to a future version of yourself, one who has successfully overcome this triggering situation. What would this wiser future self tell you? What advice would they give you to handle the present moment? This perspective can help you see beyond the immediate intensity of your emotions and make decisions more aligned with your long-term values.

Another powerful strategy is "trigger reframing." Instead of seeing the trigger as a threat, try to view it as an opportunity for learning and growth. Ask yourself: "What can I learn from this situation? How can I use this experience to become more resilient?"

The practice of "radical compassion" towards yourself is crucial in these moments. Remember that being triggered is not a sign of weakness or failure. It's a natural part of the human experience. Treat yourself with the same kindness and understanding you would offer a dear friend in distress.

A practical exercise to develop this compassion is to write a letter to yourself from a self-compassionate perspective every time you get triggered. Acknowledge the pain you're experiencing, offer words of comfort and encouragement, and remind yourself that this experience, however difficult, is temporary.

Finally, consider the importance of creating a "trigger action plan." This plan should include concrete steps to follow when you feel triggered, such as temporarily removing yourself from the situation, practicing grounding techniques, or contacting a support person. Having a predefined plan can give you a sense of control and direction in moments of intense emotion.

Chapter 5:
The Blindspot Repeating Relationship Mistakes

The psychological "blind spot" refers to an area of our self-awareness that remains hidden and inaccessible to our direct observation. This concept pertains to those behaviors, thoughts, and emotional patterns that influence our actions and decisions without our conscious realization. Recognizing its existence is crucial because it often represents the root of our recurring relational problems. Despite our efforts at self-reflection and improvement, the blind spot can cause us to repeatedly make the same mistakes, especially in intimate relationships.

The natural tendency during personal reflection is to focus on visible and tangible behaviors and events. We question what we did well and what we did wrong, trying to identify the actions that led to certain consequences. However, this analysis often overlooks hidden behaviors, those we cannot see because they are rooted in our subconscious. These hidden behaviors reside in our blind spot and are essential to recognize in order to break the cycle of repetitive mistakes.

To better understand this concept, we can use the metaphor of a tricycle. Imagine riding a tricycle with two back wheels. One of the wheels is completely flat, while the other is only partially inflated. When we try to correct our mistakes without acknowledging the blind spot, it's like trying to inflate the wheel that is already partially inflated while ignoring the completely flat one. As a result, the tricycle keeps going in circles, unable to move in a straight line. This cycle represents our inability to see and correct the hidden behaviors that hold us back.

The flat tire, in the tricycle metaphor, symbolizes those behaviors that are outside our awareness. For individuals with an anxious attachment style, these behaviors might include the tendency to excessively worry about others' actions, constantly seek external validation, and sacrifice their own needs to maintain peace in the relationship. These behaviors are often automatic and deeply rooted, making them difficult to recognize without deliberate and focused introspection.

Recognizing and understanding the psychological "blind spot" is fundamental to breaking the cycles of repetitive mistakes in relationships. Only by addressing these hidden behaviors can we hope to create lasting and positive changes in our interactions with others.

Vulnerability

If you have an anxious attachment style, you possess a distinctive strength: openness to change and growth through love. This characteristic allows you to approach relationships with a rare and precious emotional availability. You enter a relationship with an open heart, ready to learn and grow with your partner. This openness is not just a willingness to embrace the other person but also a readiness to question your own beliefs and transform through the interaction with the other.

You show remarkable vulnerability in relationships. This vulnerability manifests as a deep desire to connect and a propensity to share intimate emotions and thoughts. You are ready to bare yourself, hoping that this transparency will lead to mutual understanding and a profound bond. This approach, although it may seem risky, is driven by the belief that through openness and sincerity, you can achieve an authentic and lasting connection.

In contrast, people with an avoidant attachment style exhibit the opposite behavior. They tend to protect themselves from potential emotional harm by maintaining a certain emotional distance from their partners. This style makes it difficult for them to learn through love, as they are less inclined to show vulnerability and embrace change. While you seek closeness as a form of security, avoidants find security in independence and self-sufficiency, avoiding emotional dependence on others.

However, excessive vulnerability can pose dangers. In your quest for connection, you might find yourself revealing too much too soon, without ensuring that the other person is trustworthy or capable of responding appropriately. This premature exposure can leave you unprotected and vulnerable to emotional wounds. Your openness, if not balanced with adequate protection and the ability to set boundaries, can lead you to situations where you feel exploited or unappreciated.

Balancing Vulnerability and Self-Protection in Relationships

In relationships, finding a balance between vulnerability and self-protection is essential. Vulnerability allows for deep and authentic connections, but without adequate protection, it can lead to feeling hurt or exploited. It is crucial to learn how to protect yourself and establish personal boundaries to maintain your emotional well-being.

During childhood, caregivers and parents play a critical role in teaching us how to balance these two aspects. Through interactions with them, we learn when it is safe to be vulnerable and when it is necessary to defend ourselves. This process includes learning emotional regulation and the ability to recognize and establish healthy boundaries. If these teachings are lacking or inadequate, we may grow up struggling to balance vulnerability and protection as adults.

As adults, we are responsible for maintaining this balance. We can no longer rely solely on caregivers to protect us; we must learn to do it ourselves. This means developing the ability to assess situations and people, understanding when it is safe to open up and when it is better to maintain some emotional distance. It is a process that requires self-awareness and emotional insight, as well as the ability to adapt to circumstances flexibly.

Emotional regulation plays a fundamental role in this balance. Recognizing and managing your emotions allows you to establish and maintain healthy boundaries. Emotional regulation involves calming yourself in moments of stress, expressing your needs and desires clearly and respectfully, and recognizing when a situation is becoming too difficult to handle. Establishing healthy boundaries means knowing what is acceptable for you and what is not, and being able to communicate these limits to others effectively.

Balancing vulnerability and self-protection in relationships is not just a matter of emotional survival but also personal growth. Through this balance, we can create authentic and fulfilling relationships, where there is room for deep connection without losing our sense of self. Being vulnerable requires courage, but knowing when and how to protect yourself is equally important for building healthy and lasting relationships.

Personal Responsibility in Relationships

Imagine entering a new relationship feeling fully aware of your limits and needs. This awareness allows you to establish a solid foundation for clear and open communication with your partner. It's not enough to just know your boundaries; effectively communicating them is essential for building a healthy and respectful relationship. Clearly stating what is acceptable and what is not can prevent misunderstandings and future conflicts.

Another common challenge for those with an anxious attachment style is the tendency to seek a "savior" in their partner. Relying too heavily on the other person to feel complete or resolved can create a dependency dynamic that pressures both parties. Hoping that your partner can solve all your emotional problems is unrealistic and often leads to disappointment. This expectation is not only unfair to your partner, but it can also hinder your development of true emotional autonomy.

Taking personal responsibility is crucial to avoiding the repetition of past relationship mistakes. Recognizing your behavioral patterns and actively working to change them is the first step toward more balanced relationships. For example, if you tend to sacrifice too much of yourself to please others, it's important to be aware of this pattern and start setting healthier boundaries. Personal responsibility also means accepting your emotional reactions and striving to improve them.

To better identify your priorities and establish personal boundaries, an effective exercise is to imagine a life without a partner. Reflect on how you would spend your time, which platonic relationships you would cultivate, and what personal goals you would pursue. This type of reflection can help you understand what is truly important to you and strengthen your identity independently of a romantic partner.

Visualizing an autonomous life should not be seen as giving up on love, but rather as a way to reinforce your identity and autonomy. Knowing yourself and what you desire puts you in a better position to enter a relationship with balance and healthy boundaries, creating fertile ground for an authentic and respectful connection.

Building a Solid Identity and Healthy Boundaries

To build a solid identity, it is essential to develop a strong self-awareness and understand what truly matters in your life. This awareness allows you to clearly define who you are and what you desire, which are crucial elements for establishing effective boundaries that protect your personal integrity.

Clearly defining who you are involves identifying your core values and priorities. This clarity helps you set boundaries that reflect your true essence and protect you from situations that could compromise your emotional well-being. Without this definition, boundaries can become vague and ineffective, exposing you to harmful relational dynamics.

An important step is recognizing the significance of platonic relationships in strengthening your identity. Solid friendships and family bonds provide essential emotional support and a sense of belonging. These relationships offer opportunities to explore and affirm who you are in a safe and accepting environment.

Similarly, dedicating time to individual activities that you are passionate about contributes to cultivating your skills and personal interests. Whether it's hobbies, sports, or creative projects, these activities help you develop a deeper understanding of yourself and reinforce your identity independently of romantic relationships.

Moreover, maintaining personal integrity within relationships requires adopting effective strategies. Being aware of your emotions and reactions allows you to respond thoughtfully to situations, preventing you from compromising your boundaries. Communicating your limits and needs clearly and respectfully is fundamental for building relationships based on mutual respect and understanding.

In this way, you can develop a solid identity that enables you to establish and maintain healthy boundaries, laying the foundation for balanced and fulfilling relationships.

Share Your Thoughts

"The first step toward change is awareness. The second step is acceptance." — Nathaniel Branden

For many people, recognizing they have anxious attachment is a relief. Suddenly, everything makes sense... The constant need for reassurance, the fear of abandonment, the difficulty trusting others despite your best efforts...

Before you could see your experience through the lens of anxious attachment, you probably felt isolated and misunderstood. The truth is, there are thousands of people who feel this way — we are far from alone, yet it often feels like we're the only ones "failing" to manage relationships as expected.

My intention in writing this book is not only to help you navigate the challenges you face but to help you realize you're not alone — and you can help spread this message to more people like you. Don't worry, it only requires a few minutes of your time.

By leaving a review of this book on Amazon, you'll show new readers that they're part of a large community of people with anxious attachment... and you'll point them in the direction of a resource that can really help them.

Simply by letting other readers know how this book has helped you and what they'll find inside, you'll let them know that it's okay to be who they are and that there are others out there struggling with the same challenges.

Not only that, but you'll show them exactly where they can find the help they need without having to do anything more than click a button.

Thank you so much for your support. People with anxious attachment are often misunderstood... Together we can instigate a change.

Scan to leave a review on
Amazon if you live in the US

Scan to leave a review on
Amazon if you live in the UK

Scan to leave a review on
Amazon if you live in Canada

Scan to leave a review on
Amazon if you live in Australia

Chapter 6:
Navigating Conflict With An Anxiously Attached Partner

Understanding and improving relationship dynamics begins with identifying both your own and your partner's attachment styles. Attachment theory, which includes styles such as secure, avoidant, disorganized, and anxious, provides a framework for understanding emotional and behavioral responses in intimate relationships. Recognizing which attachment style you and your partner fall into offers a clear insight into the dynamics influencing your relationship.

The goal of attachment theory should not be merely self-analysis but practical application to improve the quality of relationships. Understanding how others operate facilitates better communication and problem-solving. For example, recognizing that an anxiously attached partner fears abandonment can help in reassuring them during conflicts, preventing the situation from worsening.

Clearing communication clutter is crucial for addressing core issues in relationships. Often, conflicts involve discussions that circle around problems without ever addressing the heart of the matter. This leads to prolonged discussions that resolve nothing. It's important to use attachment theory to clear away unnecessary distractions and focus on the real issues. For instance, a discussion can easily derail if it starts to involve secondary or past issues instead of remaining focused on the current problem.

The suggested techniques are often more easily applied by individuals with a secure attachment style, who have a greater ability to self-regulate in intense situations and remain present and empathetic during emotional conversations. However, even those with insecure attachment styles can learn and apply these techniques with practice and effort. For example, an anxiously attached person can work on managing their anxiety during conflict by practicing mindfulness and calming techniques such as deep breathing.

For those with insecure attachment styles, it's helpful to identify personal emotional triggers and develop strategies to return to calm. Recognizing moments of heightened anxiety and taking a moment to breathe deeply before responding can make a significant difference. Additionally, openly communicating needs and boundaries with a partner can prevent conflict escalation. For instance, clarifying the need for a break from the discussion to reflect and return more calmly can help manage the situation better.

Attachment theory offers valuable tools for improving communication and problem-solving in relationships. While some techniques may require more practice for those with insecure attachment styles, with dedication and awareness, it is possible to significantly enhance the quality of relational interactions, leading to healthier and more satisfying relationships.

Managing Conflicts with Anxiously Attached Partners

Managing conflicts with partners who have an anxious attachment style requires a deep understanding of their fears and emotional needs. The fear of abandonment is a central element in conflicts with these partners and can significantly amplify tensions. During a conflict, a partner with an anxious attachment may interpret any sign of disagreement or distance as an imminent threat of abandonment. This fear, if not recognized and addressed, can lead to intense emotional reactions and difficulties in resolving the conflict.

Reassuring the anxious partner during the conflict is crucial to prevent the fear of abandonment from taking over. An effective way to do this is by starting the conflict with a clear statement of intent.

For example, clearly expressing the desire to resolve the issue and reassuring the partner of your presence and commitment to the relationship can make a big difference. Phrases like "I want to resolve this problem with you because our relationship is important to me" or "I'm not going anywhere, I just want to find a solution together" can help to calm the partner's anxiety.

This initial statement serves to establish a safe ground, allowing the anxious partner to feel less threatened and more open to a constructive discussion. When an anxious partner feels that the relationship is not in danger, they are more likely to address the conflict in a calmer and more rational manner. Additionally, this ongoing reassurance can prevent the conflict from escalating, keeping the discussion focused on the real issue rather than the fear of abandonment.

Another important aspect is being aware of non-verbal signals during the conflict. Maintaining gentle eye contact, using a calm tone of voice, and adopting an open and relaxed posture can further reassure the anxious partner. These non-verbal cues communicate empathy and presence, which are crucial for maintaining a constructive dialogue.

When managing a conflict with an anxiously attached partner, it is helpful to take regular breaks to check on their emotional state. Questions like "How are you feeling right now?" or "Is there anything I can do to help you feel safer?" demonstrate attention and care, further reinforcing the partner's sense of security. It is also important to be patient and willing to listen without interrupting, giving the partner time to express their concerns and feelings.

Additionally, recognizing and validating the partner's emotions without minimizing or dismissing them is essential. Even if the anxious partner's fears seem irrational, they are real to them and deeply influence their behavior. Phrases like "I understand that you are scared that I might leave you, but I want to reassure you that it is not my intention" can help to validate their feelings and reduce anxiety.

Finally, it is useful to agree on strategies together for handling future conflicts. For example, establishing pause signals or methods for taking space when emotions become too intense can help to prevent escalation. Having a shared plan on how to manage conflicts gives the anxious partner an additional sense of security and control, helping to manage their fears and improve the overall quality of the relationship.

Triggers, Boundaries, and Space

Recognizing your own emotional triggers is a fundamental step in effectively managing conflicts in relationships. Triggers are intense emotional reactions that are activated in response to certain situations or behaviors and can negatively influence the dynamics of a conflict. Identifying these personal triggers helps maintain calm and clarity during discussions. For example, a person may recognize that they feel particularly vulnerable when criticized, which can lead them to react defensively or aggressively.

Once triggers are identified, it is essential to communicate your boundaries to your partner clearly and respectfully. This process involves clarifying what you are willing to tolerate and what you are not, and establishing limits that protect your emotional well-being. For instance, you might say, "When I feel criticized, I need to take a moment to collect my thoughts before responding." Communicating these boundaries helps prevent misunderstandings and reduces the risk of escalation during conflicts.

Communicating boundaries must be done with tact and sensitivity to avoid making your partner feel rejected or attacked. Using "I" statements, such as "I feel" or "I need," can make communication more effective and less accusatory. For example, instead of saying,

"Stop criticizing me," you could say, "I feel overwhelmed when I receive criticism and need a moment to reflect."

Taking space when necessary is another crucial tool for preventing the escalation of conversations. During a conflict, emotions can become overwhelming, making it difficult to maintain calm and clarity. In these moments, it is helpful to pause the discussion and return with a calmer and more reflective mind. For instance, you might tell your partner, "I need to take a 15-minute break to calm down, and then we can resume the conversation."

This practice not only helps reduce immediate tension but also allows for better reflection on your feelings and needs. It is important to communicate clearly that the break is temporary and that you intend to return to the discussion. This reassures your partner and reduces the fear of abandonment or avoiding the issue.

Practical strategies for pausing the conflict include deep breathing techniques, short walks, or any activity that helps you regain calm. During this time, reflecting on your triggers and boundaries can better prepare you for a more productive and less emotionally charged discussion.

When returning to the conversation, it is helpful to restart with a statement of intent, reaffirming the importance of the relationship and the desire to resolve the issue together. This approach reinforces collaboration and mutual understanding, allowing for more effective conflict resolution.

Managing triggers, communicating boundaries, and the ability to take space when necessary are all key elements for improving the quality of relationships and resolving conflicts constructively. These practices require awareness and commitment but can lead to greater understanding and harmony within the couple.

Communicating Triggers to Your Partner

Establishing clear boundaries and communicating your triggers to your partner is crucial for effectively managing conflicts in relationships. When boundaries are not clearly defined, it's easy for your partner's behaviors to be perceived as invasive or disrespectful, leading to intense emotional reactions. Letting your partner know which behaviors are acceptable and which are not helps create a healthier and more respectful relational environment.

To prevent conflict from escalating, it's essential to communicate boundaries clearly and promptly. For example, you might say, "When you raise your voice, I feel very uncomfortable and can't think clearly. I would prefer that we speak in calmer tones." This type of communication not only informs your partner of your limits but also helps them understand the impact of their behaviors on your emotions.

Taking a break from the conflict when necessary is another effective strategy to avoid escalation. During an argument, emotions can become so intense that it becomes difficult to remain calm and clear-headed. Taking a break allows tempers to cool and gives you a chance to return to the discussion with a more reflective and less reactive perspective. For instance, you might say, "I feel like I'm about to lose my temper; I need to take a few minutes to gather my thoughts."

Clearly communicating your triggers to your partner is equally important. This involves explaining which situations or behaviors trigger intense emotional reactions. For example, you might say, "When I see you using your phone during an important discussion, I feel ignored, and it makes me very angry." This communication helps your partner better understand your emotional reactions, facilitating more effective management of relational dynamics.

It's crucial that these communications are not accusatory but are instead oriented toward mutual understanding and problem-solving. Using language that avoids blaming and focuses instead on your feelings can make a significant difference. For example, instead of saying, "You always do this, and it makes me angry," you could say, "I feel frustrated when this happens because it seems like you're not listening to me." This approach helps keep the communication open and constructive, avoiding defensive reactions from your partner.

Additionally, it's helpful to establish communication methods that allow you to manage triggers proactively. For example, agreeing on a signal that indicates the need for a break or a method to express your feelings without interrupting the flow of conversation can help keep the dialogue productive. These methods might include phrases like, "I feel like I'm reaching my limit, can we take a break?" or using agreed-upon gestures to indicate the need for space.

Finally, creating a safe space where both parties feel free to express their feelings and needs without fear of judgment or retaliation is essential. This safe space fosters open and honest dialogue, allowing both partners to explore and better understand each other's emotional reactions. Once this environment is established, it's possible to address conflicts in a calmer and more collaborative manner, improving the overall quality of the relationship.

Recognizing Feelings Without Agreeing With the Logic

Recognizing and validating your partner's feelings is fundamental to improving communication and managing conflicts in relationships, especially when dealing with individuals who have an anxious attachment style. These individuals tend to perceive their feelings as absolute reality, even when the logic behind them may be distorted. This can lead to situations where your partner's feelings seem exaggerated or irrational, but it's important to remember that for them, these feelings are real and valid.

Emotional validation is the process of acknowledging and accepting someone else's feelings without necessarily agreeing with the logic that underpins them. For example, if your partner expresses fear that you might leave them due to an innocuous behavior, you can acknowledge their pain without accepting the premise that you will actually leave. You could say something like, "I understand that you feel scared and insecure right now, and I'm sorry that you're experiencing these emotions. I want to reassure you that I have no intention of leaving you."

This type of response allows your partner to feel understood and heard, reducing the intensity of their negative emotions. Validating feelings doesn't mean admitting that your partner's fears or concerns are justified, but rather recognizing that these emotions exist and have a real impact on their experience.

Another practical example might be during a discussion where your partner feels neglected. Even if you believe you've been attentive, you can still acknowledge their feelings by saying, "I understand that you feel neglected and that this makes you feel bad. I'm sorry you feel this way and I want to do my best to ensure you don't feel this way in the future." This way, you validate their feelings without necessarily agreeing with their interpretation of your behavior.

It's also important to clearly distinguish between feelings and logic. For instance, your partner might say, "You don't love me because you don't spend enough time with me." In this situation, you can validate their feelings without agreeing with the logic by saying, "I hear that you feel unloved, and I appreciate you telling me. My lack of time doesn't reflect a lack of love, but I understand it may seem that way, and I'll work on improving this."

Recognizing feelings without agreeing with the logic is an effective conflict management strategy, as it reduces the need to be defensive or justify yourself, allowing you to focus on the emotional aspect of the problem. This approach can help to calm tensions and create a more open and safe communication environment.

The art of emotional validation requires practice and sensitivity. It is essential to actively listen to your partner, showing empathy and understanding, and responding in a way that makes them feel genuinely heard and supported. Through this process, you can build a stronger and more resilient relationship, where both partners feel respected and understood.

Additionally, it is helpful to maintain clear and non-accusatory language during validation. Avoiding phrases like "You shouldn't feel that way" or "You're overreacting" helps prevent your partner from feeling invalidated or judged. Instead, phrases like "I understand that this situation makes you feel this way" or "It's understandable that you feel this way" can make a big difference in helping your partner feel accepted and respected.

Chapter 7:
Conflict Management Strategies

Why do some people react to emotional difficulties with such intensity, while others seem to withdraw into their shells? The answers to these questions often lie in the attachment styles developed during childhood. A person's attachment style profoundly influences how they perceive and manage interpersonal relationships and, consequently, how they handle conflicts.

People with an anxious attachment style tend to experience their world through a highly intense emotional filter. When faced with conflict, their primary reaction is to communicate how they feel. Their world is heavily influenced by emotions, and these emotions often become their measure of reality. It's not uncommon for them to exaggerate their feelings, desperately trying to gain the understanding and attention of their partner. This exaggeration isn't a conscious attempt to manipulate reality but rather a way to ensure their emotional pain is recognized and validated.

On the other end of the spectrum are people with an avoidant attachment style. These individuals tend to organize their worldview differently, relying more on concrete facts and the chronological order of events rather than emotions. During a conflict, their focus shifts to the specific details of what happened, trying to reconstruct the sequence of events to make sense of the situation. This approach can make them seem insensitive or as if they're minimizing their partner's feelings, but in reality, they are trying to manage their own emotions through logic and analysis of the facts.

These fundamental differences can lead to significant misunderstandings. Imagine a couple where one partner has an anxious attachment style and the other an avoidant one. The anxious partner might recount a stressful work incident with great drama, seeking immediate emotional support. The avoidant partner, however, might focus on the inconsistencies in the story, trying to understand exactly what happened. This can be frustrating for both: the anxious partner feels unheard and invalidated, while the avoidant partner feels confused and overwhelmed by the perceived exaggerations.

This divergence in interpreting and reacting to events can create a cycle of conflict. The anxious partner constantly feels unheard, so they intensify their emotions in hopes of eliciting a reaction. The avoidant partner, faced with these exaggerated emotional expressions, withdraws further, seeking refuge in logic and facts, thereby worsening the anxious partner's sense of loneliness and misunderstanding.

Understanding these differences is the first step towards improving communication and conflict management in relationships. People with an anxious attachment need to learn to express their emotions more clearly and directly without exaggerating the facts. They also need to understand that their avoidant partner isn't dismissing their feelings but is simply using a different method to deal with the situation.

At the same time, people with an avoidant attachment need to work on being more empathetic and recognizing the importance of emotions in the communication process. They should try to listen to their partner's feelings without focusing too much on the concrete details, offering validation and emotional support.

The key lies in finding a balance between these two approaches, creating common ground where both emotions and facts can be discussed openly and with mutual respect. Only through this mutual understanding and adaptation can stronger and more satisfying relationships be built.

The Role of Emotions in Conflicts

During an argument, have you ever noticed how some people seem to explode in a sea of emotions, while others maintain a cool, detached attitude? These contrasting reactions often reflect their attachment styles. Emotions play a crucial role in conflicts, especially between individuals with anxious and avoidant attachment styles.

For those with an anxious attachment style, emotions are the prism through which every event is interpreted. When they feel ignored or misunderstood, these individuals tend to exaggerate their emotions. For example, if their partner doesn't show enough empathy after a stressful day, the anxious person might dramatize the event, describing it as a huge injustice to elicit an emotional reaction. This behavior stems from a desperate need to feel seen and understood.

This exaggeration can create inconsistencies in their narratives. Stories told by a person with an anxious attachment can appear incoherent because their perception is distorted by the intense emotions they are experiencing. This distortion is not intentional; it's an emotional survival mechanism aimed at communicating the depth of their pain and frustration.

On the other hand, people with an avoidant attachment style handle conflicts very differently. For them, concrete details and the chronological order of events are fundamental to understanding the situation. Returning to the example of the couple, the avoidant partner might focus on exactly what was said and done, trying to reconstruct the timeline to understand where the problem originated. This approach can make the avoidant seem like they are minimizing the anxious partner's feelings when, in reality, they are trying to make logical sense of the situation.

These different ways of handling conflicts can lead to profound misunderstandings. The anxious partner, seeing that the avoidant is focusing only on facts and not on emotions, will feel further ignored and misunderstood. At the same time, the avoidant might interpret the anxious partner's emotional exaggerations as irrational and out of place, increasing their frustration.

A practical example of these dynamics could be a discussion about a household chore, like dividing tasks. The anxious partner might feel overwhelmed and express their discomfort with great emotional intensity, possibly exaggerating the problem. The avoidant, instead, might try to analyze when and how each task was done, losing sight of the anxious partner's perceived injustice.

To improve conflict management, it is essential that both parties understand the importance of emotions. People with anxious attachment need to learn to communicate their feelings more directly and less exaggeratedly. They should try to explain to their partner exactly how they feel without resorting to dramatizations that can confuse.

An effective strategy might be using phrases like, "I feel hurt when I don't get your attention after a difficult day." This type of direct communication helps clarify feelings without exaggerating facts. Additionally, practicing self-awareness techniques, like keeping an emotional journal, can help the anxious person identify and regulate their emotions before communicating them.

Similarly, people with avoidant attachment need to make a conscious effort to recognize and validate the anxious partner's emotions. Instead of focusing exclusively on facts, they should try to understand the emotional context and offer empathy. This doesn't mean ignoring concrete details, but balancing them with attention to the other's emotions.

A useful technique could be asking open-ended questions that encourage the anxious partner to express their feelings, such as, "Can you tell me more about how you're feeling about this?" This type of question demonstrates empathy and interest in the partner's emotions, facilitating more balanced communication.

It is this balance between emotions and facts that can lead to more effective communication and more satisfying conflict resolution. When both partners acknowledge and respect both feelings and concrete details, they can work together to overcome misunderstandings and strengthen their relationship.

Communication Strategies for the Anxious Partner

Have you ever felt the need to shout to be heard? To amplify your pain, hoping that the intensity of your words will make your partner understand how much you are suffering? For people with an anxious attachment style, this experience is common. Often, in an attempt to be understood, they exaggerate their emotions, creating misunderstandings and conflicts. But how can you communicate effectively without falling into these exaggerations?

The first fundamental strategy is to recognize your emotional state. Often, those with an anxious attachment can feel overwhelmed by their emotions without understanding exactly what they are experiencing. Taking a moment to reflect on what you are truly feeling can make a big difference. For example, you might ask yourself: "Am I really feeling anger, or is it more a sense of sadness and abandonment?" Identifying the emotion precisely is the first step to communicating it clearly.

Once you have recognized your emotions, it is important to communicate them directly and honestly. Instead of exaggerating or distorting the facts to get a reaction, try to express exactly how you feel. Phrases like "I feel sad when you don't respond to my messages" are much more effective than "You never respond to my messages, and this shows that you don't care about me." The first phrase communicates a specific feeling and allows your partner to understand your emotional state without feeling attacked or blamed.

Another useful technique is keeping an emotional journal. Writing down your emotions and the situations that triggered them can help identify recurring patterns and develop greater self-awareness. This exercise can be particularly useful before addressing a delicate conversation with your partner. Knowing what to say and how to say it, having already reflected on it, can make communication smoother and less tense.

The practice of active listening is equally important. Although it may seem contradictory, learning to listen carefully to your partner can significantly improve your communication skills. When the other person feels heard and understood, they are more likely to respond with empathy and understanding. During a conversation, try to repeat what your partner has said in your own words to ensure you have correctly understood their point of view. Phrases like "So, if I understand correctly, you feel frustrated because..." can show that you are genuinely listening and trying to understand.

Finally, it is helpful to establish communication rules within the relationship. These might include a commitment not to interrupt each other while speaking, not using accusatory language, and taking a break if the conversation becomes too heated. Establishing these rules during a calm moment, away from any conflict, can help both partners feel more secure and respected during discussions.

Communicating effectively requires practice and awareness. Changing deeply ingrained habits is not always easy, but with time and effort, it is possible to develop a healthier and more constructive communication style. Remember, the goal is not to avoid conflicts entirely but to manage them in a way that strengthens the relationship and increases mutual understanding.

Communication Strategies for the Avoidant Partner

If you have an anxious attachment style, you might often feel frustrated or misunderstood during conflicts with your avoidant partner. Your need to express emotions intensely can seem at odds with your partner's more detached approach. How can you improve communication and help your partner understand you better without focusing excessively on concrete details?

The first strategy is to help your partner recognize the importance of your emotions. Even when your narrative of events may seem exaggerated or inconsistent, it's crucial for your partner to learn to validate your feelings. You can explain that your pain and frustration are real and that you need to feel heard. Phrases like, "I need you to acknowledge how upset I am" can be a good starting point to convey the importance of your emotions.

Encouraging your partner to practice empathetic listening can significantly improve communication. Explain that you need them to listen without interrupting or judging, trying to understand what you are truly feeling. Instead of focusing immediately on the details of your story, your partner should reflect on the feelings you are expressing. Phrases like, "It seems like you're feeling frustrated because..." can help demonstrate that they are genuinely listening and trying to understand your emotional state.

You can also suggest that your partner ask open-ended questions that encourage you to express your emotions more deeply. Questions like, "Can you explain more about what made you feel this way?" or "What do you think could help you feel better right now?" can facilitate more open and less defensive communication. These questions show that your partner is interested not just in the facts but also in your emotions and experiences.

It's also important to balance the understanding of facts with empathy for your emotions. Explain to your partner that while it's natural for them to want to organize the sequence of events, your emotions don't always follow a linear logic. Trying to resolve the conflict solely through the analysis of facts can lead to further emotional distance. Integrating the understanding of facts with an empathetic approach can help bridge the gap between your perspectives.

Finally, work together to establish a safe communication environment. Make sure both of you feel free to express your feelings without fear of judgment or retaliation. You can agree to take breaks during heated discussions or commit to not using accusatory language. Creating a space of mutual respect and listening can foster healthier and more constructive communication.

Dealing with conflicts with an avoidant partner requires patience and understanding from both sides. It's not enough to focus only on concrete details; it's also necessary to recognize and validate emotions to build more balanced and satisfying communication.

Growth and Conflict Resolution

Managing conflicts in relationships, especially between partners with different attachment styles, requires a conscious and collaborative approach. Here are some practical techniques that can help improve communication and find common ground.

To begin, it's important to create a safe communication environment. Both partners need to feel free to express their feelings without fear of judgment or criticism. Establish basic rules together, such as avoiding interruptions and taking breaks if the discussion becomes too heated. This can help keep the conversation constructive and respectful.

Another effective technique is practicing active listening. Listening carefully to your partner without interrupting or judging can make a big difference. For example, repeat what you've understood in your own words to ensure you've grasped their point of view correctly. Phrases like, "If I understand correctly, you feel frustrated because..." show that you are truly listening and trying to understand their emotions.

Incorporating weekly reflection moments can also be helpful. Set aside a fixed time each week to discuss your emotions, needs, and unresolved conflicts. This can be an opportunity to express feelings that may have been suppressed and to work together on resolving conflicts constructively.

For personal growth, mindfulness can be a powerful tool. Learning to be present in the moment and observing your emotions without judgment helps manage stress and anxiety better. Short sessions of meditation or mindful breathing exercises can be very beneficial.

In the context of the relationship, it's essential to integrate the understanding of facts with empathy for emotions. This means that while it's important to consider the concrete details of a situation, it's equally important to recognize and validate your partner's emotions. A good balance between these two aspects can help avoid misunderstandings and build stronger communication.

Finally, adopting a collaborative approach to problem-solving can significantly improve conflict management. Work together to find solutions to problems, brainstorming and evaluating the pros and cons of each option. This approach not only facilitates conflict resolution but also strengthens the sense of partnership and cooperation in the relationship.

Using these techniques may take time and practice, but with commitment and patience, it's possible to develop more effective communication and resolve conflicts constructively, creating a stronger and more satisfying relationship.

Chapter 8:
The 'Worthiness Wound'

Have you ever wondered why, despite your successes, you still feel inadequate? Or why, even when you receive compliments, a voice inside whispers that you don't really deserve them? Welcome to the world of the "worthiness wound," a concept that might illuminate dark corners of your psyche you didn't even know existed.

Imagine having a lens through which you view the world, but this lens is slightly distorted. Everything you observe - your relationships, your successes, even your reflection in the mirror - is filtered through this imperfect lens. This is the essence of the worthiness wound: a distortion in the perception of your intrinsic value that colors every aspect of life.

But where does this wound come from? Its roots often lie in childhood, in those crucial moments when our sense of self is forming. Perhaps you were a sensitive child in a family that valued toughness. Or maybe your parents, though loving, were too caught up in their own problems to offer you the constant validation you needed. These early experiences can leave invisible scars that we carry into adulthood.

The worthiness wound is intimately connected with an anxious attachment style. Think of a child constantly seeking parental approval, always afraid of not being enough. This child grows into an adult who constantly doubts their own worth, seeking external validation to fill an inner void. It's like having a bottomless well inside, which no amount of praise or success seems able to fill.

In adult relationships, this wound manifests in subtle but pervasive ways. You might find yourself sabotaging promising relationships, convinced you don't deserve love. Or perhaps you find yourself working tirelessly, trying to prove your worth through ever-greater achievements. The sad irony is that the more you try to prove your worth to others, the further you move away from true self-acceptance.

But beware: the worthiness wound is not simply low self-esteem. It's a deeper, more pervasive phenomenon. While low self-esteem can fluctuate based on circumstances, the worthiness wound is a deep-rooted belief that influences every aspect of your life. It's like a faulty operating system running in the background, affecting every "program" you run.

Recognizing this wound is the first, crucial step towards healing. It takes courage to look within and admit that maybe, just maybe, the way we've always seen ourselves isn't the only possible truth. It's a process that can be painful, but also incredibly liberating.

Think about all the times you've held back, when you didn't dare to dream big or when you gave up before even trying. How many opportunities have you missed because of this deep-seated belief that you're not enough? The good news is that recognizing the wound is already a step towards healing it.

It's not about magically erasing years of ingrained beliefs. It's more like starting to reprogram that faulty operating system, one bit at a time. Start by observing your thoughts without judgment. Notice how you react to compliments, how you behave in stressful situations. These observations are the first building blocks for constructing a new perception of yourself.

The worthiness wound may seem like an insurmountable obstacle, but recognizing it is already an act of courage and self-love. It's the first step on a journey towards a more authentic and complete version of yourself. A journey that requires patience, self-compassion, and, above all, the willingness to see beyond that distorted lens you've used for so long.

The Awakening of Self-Worth

A New Perspective on Self: Opportunities and Obstacles

Imagine waking up one day to find that the distorted lens through which you've always viewed the world has begun to clear. It's as if a veil is lifting, allowing you to glimpse your true worth for the first time. This process of rediscovery is as exhilarating as it is unsettling.

The journey often begins with a flash of awareness. Perhaps it's a kind word from a friend that, for some reason, you're really able to hear this time. Or maybe it's an unexpected success that makes you think, "What if I am capable after all?" These moments of clarity can be sparks that ignite a fire of change.

But beware: this transformation isn't a switch that flips on suddenly. It's more like a dawn, with light gradually making its way through the darkness. At first, you might feel disoriented. The old certainties - however painful - begin to waver, and you find yourself in uncharted territory.

One of the biggest challenges at this stage is the shift from constantly seeking external validation to finding an internal source of value. It's like learning to walk again. You've always relied on others to tell you who you are and what you're worth. Now, you have to learn to do it yourself. This process can be frightening. You wonder, "If I'm not defined by others' judgments, who am I really?"

There's also the risk of falling into the trap of unrealistic expectations. Now that you've glimpsed your potential, you might expect everything to change immediately. You want a perfect relationship, a successful career, a problem-free life. But the reality is that personal growth takes time. It's a process, not an event.

Past experiences play a crucial role in this discovery phase. Memories of times when you felt inadequate or unloved may resurface. It's as if your subconscious is doing spring cleaning, bringing old pains to light that need to be addressed. This can be painful, but it's also an opportunity for true healing.

A useful strategy during this period is to start keeping a success journal. Not just big achievements, but also small daily victories. Did you make a phone call you'd been putting off? Did you express your opinion in a meeting? These are important steps. Writing them down helps you build a new narrative about yourself.

Another powerful exercise is the "mirror" technique. Every morning, look in the mirror and say something positive to yourself. At first, it might seem ridiculous or fake. But over time, these affirmations begin to take root. You're literally reprogramming your internal dialogue.

As your self-perception grows, you might notice changes in your relationships. Some people might react positively to your new sense of worth. Others might feel threatened or uncomfortable. It's important to remember that this is your journey. Not everyone will understand or approve, and that's okay.

This path of self-discovery is like learning a new language. At first, you make a lot of mistakes. You feel clumsy and insecure. But with practice, it becomes more natural. You start thinking in this new language of self-acceptance and self-love.

Remember, this isn't about becoming arrogant or narcissistic. A healthy self-regard doesn't mean believing you're better than others. It means recognizing your intrinsic worth, regardless of external successes or failures.

As you navigate these uncharted waters of your new sense of self, be kind to yourself. There will be days when the old distorted lens seems to return. Days when you doubt your worth again. But now you have the tools to recognize these thoughts for what they are: echoes of old wounds, not absolute truths.

This journey of rediscovery is ongoing, not a final destination. It's a continuous process of exploration and re-exploration of self. With each step, with each challenge overcome, you're building a stronger foundation on which to base your life. And from this foundation, you can finally begin to explore your true potential, free from the chains of the worthiness wound.

The Importance of Competence

"I believe in myself!" you exclaim enthusiastically, finally feeling free from the weight of insecurity. But then comes the moment of truth: you face a real challenge, and suddenly you realize that self-confidence alone isn't enough. Welcome to the uncharted territory beyond the boundaries of self-esteem, where competence becomes the key to turning potential into reality.

There's a crucial distinction between self-esteem and self-efficacy. Self-esteem is like the emotional fuel that drives you to act, but self-efficacy is the actual ability to steer the vehicle of your life. You can feel worthy and deserving (self-esteem), but if you lack the skills necessary to face life's challenges (self-efficacy), you might still find yourself stuck.

Think of this concept as the difference between being at the starting line of a race and actually winning the competition. Self-esteem gets you to the starting point, gives you the courage to put yourself out there. But to win the race, you need training, strategy, and concrete skills. This is the essence of self-efficacy.

Many people, after working hard on their self-esteem, find themselves frustrated because life doesn't magically change. They wonder, "Why, even though I feel more confident, am I still not getting the results I want?" The answer lies in the fact that feeling worthy is only half the equation. The other half is developing practical skills to navigate the real world.

Developing skills requires commitment, time, and inevitably, a willingness to make mistakes. This can be particularly difficult for those who have struggled with self-esteem issues. The fear of failing and confirming old negative beliefs about oneself can be paralyzing. But this is where the true strength of self-esteem comes into play: it allows you to see mistakes not as confirmations of your low worth, but as opportunities for learning and growth.

A practical approach to balancing self-esteem and skill development is to set gradual goals. Instead of aspiring to immediate radical transformations, focus on small, achievable steps. Want to improve your communication skills? Start by practicing in low-risk situations, maybe in a support group or with trusted friends. Gradually increase the difficulty of the challenges you face.

It's crucial to remember that skill development is an ongoing process. There's no definitive endpoint. Even the most established experts continue to learn and improve. This awareness can be liberating: you don't have to be perfect, you just need to be willing to continuously grow.

A useful exercise is to create a "skill map." Identify areas of your life where you'd like to improve. Then, for each area, list the specific skills needed. This will give you a clear vision of what you need to work on, transforming vague goals into concrete action plans.

Remember, self-efficacy isn't just about technical skills, but also emotional and relational ones. Learning to manage stress, communicate effectively, resolve conflicts are all vital skills that can be developed with practice.

Finally, celebrate your progress, no matter how small it may seem. Every new skill acquired, every challenge overcome is a step forward in your growth journey. These successes not only strengthen your self-esteem but also build a tangible sense of competence that no one can take away from you.

Remember, the goal isn't perfection, but progress. With each new skill you acquire, you not only become more capable, but you also strengthen your belief that you can face any challenge life presents. This is the true power that comes from combining healthy self-esteem with solid skills: confidence not just in who you are, but in what you can do.

Balancing the Inner and Outer Worlds

Have you ever noticed how some people seem to glow from within, yet struggle to transform that light into concrete actions in the real world? Or, conversely, individuals who appear to have everything under control externally, but feel empty inside? This paradox brings us to the heart of one of the most complex challenges in the journey of personal growth: balancing our inner world with the outer one.

Inner work - building self-esteem, self-understanding, managing emotions - is fundamental. But if it remains confined to our minds, it risks turning into an ivory tower, beautiful but isolated from daily reality. On the other hand, focusing exclusively on external actions and results without cultivating our inner selves can lead to a sense of emptiness and dissatisfaction.

The key lies in integration. Imagine you're an artist: your inner vision is the source of inspiration, but it's your concrete actions - the movement of the brush on canvas, the choice of colors, the technique refined through practice - that transform that vision into a tangible work of art. Similarly, your inner work provides direction and energy, while your actions in the external world give shape and substance to your dreams and values.

A common trap in this process is inner perfectionism. You might think you need to completely resolve every emotional issue before acting in the world. But the truth is that personal growth and external action feed each other. Every step you take outside your comfort zone, every interaction with the world, offers you new perspectives on yourself and new opportunities for growth.

To concretely apply your personal growth in daily life, start with small experiments. If you've been working on your assertiveness, try expressing an opinion in a work meeting. If you're developing your self-esteem, challenge yourself to try a new activity in public. These "life experiments" allow you to test and strengthen your inner progress in a real context.

Relationships represent a particularly fertile ground for this balance. As you grow internally, you might notice changes in how you interact with others. Perhaps you feel more confident in expressing your needs or more capable of setting healthy boundaries. At the same time, others' reactions to your new ways of interacting offer valuable feedback for your ongoing personal development.

A crucial aspect of this balancing act is managing expectations. Inner change takes time to fully manifest in the outer world. You might feel different internally, but people around you might still react based on the "old version" of you. Patience and persistence are essential. Continue to act in line with your new self, even when the external world seems not to notice immediately.

The balance between vulnerability and self-protection is another key element. Opening up to the world and relationships always involves some degree of risk. The challenge lies in finding the right balance between showing your true essence and maintaining healthy boundaries. This doesn't mean wearing a mask, but rather consciously choosing how much and in what way to share yourself with others.

A practical exercise to work on this balance is the "integration diary." Every day, note down a concrete action you've taken that reflects your inner work. Then, reflect on how this action has affected your environment and relationships, and how external reactions have in turn influenced your inner state. This will help you see more clearly the connections between your inner and outer worlds.

Strategies for Personal and Relational Growth

The journey of personal growth is like climbing a mountain without a precise map. Each step reveals new challenges, unexpected vistas, and alternative paths. But with the right strategies, this climb can transform from a daunting task into an exciting and rewarding adventure.

Awareness is your compass on this journey. Start by observing your behavioral patterns without judgment. Notice how you react to stressful situations, how you communicate with others, how you treat yourself in difficult moments. This careful observation is the first step to dismantling ingrained habits and building new, healthier patterns of behavior.

A powerful exercise to develop this awareness is the practice of the "inner witness." During your daily interactions, imagine having a part of you that neutrally observes your thoughts, emotions, and actions. This detachment allows you to respond to situations more reflectively rather than reactively.

Emotional self-regulation is another crucial skill to cultivate. Think of your emotions as an internal thermostat: the goal isn't to eliminate "negative" emotions, but to learn to regulate their intensity. Deep breathing techniques, mindfulness meditation, or simply practicing pausing before reacting can work wonders in managing emotional storms.

Communication in relationships is often the testing ground for our personal growth. Here, active listening becomes fundamental. Practice the art of truly listening to the other person, without mentally preparing your response. Use phrases like "If I understand correctly, you're saying that..." to verify your understanding and show the other person that you're really listening.

To strengthen your personal identity and self-esteem, start keeping a "success journal." Every evening, write down three things you did well during the day, no matter how small they may seem. This exercise helps you recognize your worth and build a more positive narrative about yourself.

Integrating personal growth with professional and social development is another crucial challenge. Start seeing every interaction at work or in your social life as an opportunity to put your new skills into practice. If you're working on assertiveness, you might start by expressing your ideas in less important meetings, then gain confidence in more challenging contexts.

Resilience is a quality that develops through practice. Regularly challenge yourself to step out of your comfort zone. Start with small challenges and gradually increase the difficulty. Every time you face a difficult situation, remember to reflect not only on the outcome but also on what you learned in the process.

Gratitude is a powerful tool for transformation. Dedicate a few minutes each day to acknowledging the things you're grateful for. This simple exercise can shift your focus from what's missing in your life to what you already have, creating a more solid foundation for growth.

Finally, remember that personal growth doesn't happen in a vacuum. Actively seek feedback from people you trust. Ask them to share honest observations about the changes they notice in you. This will give you valuable information on how your inner work is manifesting in the external world.

Each of these strategies is like a tool in your personal growth toolbox. Some will work better than others in certain situations. The important thing is to experiment, adapt, and above all, be kind to yourself in the process. Personal growth is a journey, not a destination, and every step forward, no matter how small, is a victory to celebrate.

Chapter 9:
Self-Sabotage vs Attachment Wounding

Have you ever felt like an emotional yo-yo, swinging between the euphoria of reconciliation and the anguish of separation? Welcome to the world of on-off relationships, a maze of emotions where many people with anxious attachment find themselves trapped.

Imagine being on a carousel. Sometimes you're up high, feeling safe and loved. Then, suddenly, you plummet down into the darkness of loneliness and insecurity. This emotional rollercoaster is daily bread for those living in on-off relationships with anxious attachment.

But why do we find ourselves in these situations? The answer lies deep within us, in the roots of our attachment. Like an echo from the past, our desperate need for connection and reassurance resonates in every interaction. We constantly seek confirmation, as if every gesture or word from our partner were a lifeline in a sea of uncertainty.

And here's where the dance of fate comes into play: often, those with anxious attachment find themselves attracted to partners with avoidant tendencies. It's as if two pieces of a dysfunctional puzzle fit together perfectly. While the anxious desperately seeks intimacy, the avoidant withdraws, creating an endless cycle of approach and retreat.

Think about this: every time your partner pulls away, it's not just a person distancing themselves. It's as if the ground beneath your feet starts to shake, awakening ancestral fears of abandonment. Panic creeps in, and suddenly you find yourself doing everything to regain that closeness, even at the cost of sacrificing parts of yourself.

But beware: this isn't an inescapable fate. Recognizing these patterns is like turning on a light in a dark room. Suddenly, you clearly see the outlines of the furniture you kept bumping into.

Let's ask ourselves: how much of this behavior is truly love, and how much is fear masquerading as attachment? When we desperately cling to a relationship, are we really seeking the other person, or are we just trying to quell our anxieties?

The truth is that often, in trying to avoid the pain of loneliness, we find ourselves making choices that, paradoxically, cause us even more suffering. It's as if we prefer a familiar pain to a potentially liberating unknown.

But there's hope. Imagine being able to observe these dynamics from the outside, as if you were watching a movie. What would you say to the protagonist? You'd probably encourage them to take care of themselves, to establish healthy boundaries, to seek relationships that nourish instead of drain.

Well, this is exactly what you need to do now. Start treating yourself with the same compassion and wisdom you'd offer a dear friend. Recognize that your worth doesn't depend on someone else's presence or approval.

Five Crucial Questions Before Reconciling

Your phone vibrates. A message from your ex lights up the screen. Your heart races, your palms sweat. It's the moment you've been waiting for, or perhaps dreading. Before you respond, however, there's crucial work to be done: honest introspection.

Reconciling with an ex isn't a decision to be taken lightly. It's a step that requires careful consideration, self-awareness, and above all, emotional clarity. In a world where immediate impulse often prevails over reflection, taking the time to thoroughly examine your motivations might seem counterintuitive. Yet, it's precisely in these moments of pause and reflection that we can find the key to breaking dysfunctional cycles and building healthier, more fulfilling relationships.

That's why it's essential to ask yourself these five key questions:

1. *What really caused the breakup last time?*

Often, what seems obvious hides deeper truths. Don't stop at the surface. Explore the underlying patterns and dynamics. Were there communication problems? Misaligned expectations? Or perhaps you were growing in divergent directions?

This question requires deep honesty with yourself. It's easy to point fingers, blame the other person or external circumstances. But the truth is often more complex and nuanced. Maybe there were communication issues that neither of you knew how to address. Perhaps you had different expectations about the relationship that you never really articulated. Or maybe you were simply at different stages of life, with misaligned goals and desires.

Take the time to reflect on every aspect of your dynamic. Consider not just the events that led to the breakup, but also the recurring patterns in your relationship. Were there red flags you ignored? Moments when you could have acted differently?

This analysis isn't meant to induce guilt, but to provide a deeper and more objective understanding of the situation. Only by truly understanding what went wrong can you assess if and how these issues can be addressed differently in the future.

2. *What has changed since then?*

Time alone isn't a healer. Reflect on how you've grown during the separation. How have you evolved? And, just as importantly, how has your ex evolved? If the foundations remain the same, why would the building stand this time?

Change is at the heart of any meaningful reconciliation. It's not enough that time has passed; what matters is how that time was used. Have you worked on yourself? Have you sought to understand and address your dysfunctional patterns? Have you developed new emotional or communication skills?

Consider your ex's journey as well. If possible, try to understand how they've used this time apart. Have they embarked on a path of personal growth? Have they addressed the issues that contributed to the breakup?

It's crucial to be realistic. If neither of you has changed significantly, you're likely to soon find yourselves facing the same problems. Real change requires commitment, awareness, and often the help of professionals like therapists or counselors.

3. Am I going back for love or fear?

This is perhaps the most difficult question, but also the most important. Do you truly desire this specific person, or are you trying to escape loneliness? Authentic love liberates and values. Fear, on the other hand, creates anxiety and desperation. Can you recognize the difference in your heart?

Anxious attachment can make it particularly difficult to distinguish between authentic love and fear of abandonment or loneliness. Often, what we perceive as love can actually be a form of emotional dependence.

Reflect carefully on your motivations. Do you really miss this specific person, with all their peculiarities and imperfections? Or do you simply miss the idea of being in a relationship? Are you attracted to the potential of what could be, rather than the reality of what has been?

It's also important to consider how you feel when you're not with this person. Do you feel complete, capable of living a full and satisfying life on your own? Or do you feel a constant void that only the other's presence seems to fill?

Healthy love should enrich your life, not completely define it. It should make you feel secure and valued, not anxious and insecure. If you find yourself constantly needing reassurance or fearing abandonment, it might be a sign that you're acting more out of fear than authentic love.

4. *What are my non-negotiable boundaries?*

Before reconnecting, you need to be clear about who you are and what you want. What are your core values? What behaviors or situations are you no longer willing to tolerate? Setting clear boundaries isn't selfishness, it's self-respect.

Boundaries are essential for any healthy relationship, but they can be particularly challenging for those with anxious attachment. Often, there's a tendency to sacrifice one's own needs and desires for fear of losing the other.

Start by taking inventory of your fundamental values and needs. What's absolutely essential for you in a relationship? It might be mutual respect, honest communication, fidelity, or support for your personal goals.

Then, reflect on behaviors or situations you're no longer willing to accept. Perhaps in the past, you tolerated disrespect, emotional manipulation, or a constant lack of commitment. Now is the time to clearly establish your limits.

Remember, setting boundaries doesn't mean being rigid or punitive. It's about clearly communicating your needs and expectations, and being willing to enforce these limits if necessary. This clarity not only protects yourself but can also lead to a healthier and more balanced relationship.

5. *Do we have the tools to address old problems in new ways?*

The same strategies will lead to the same results. Have you acquired new communication skills? Have you learned to better manage your emotions? And your ex? If there are no new tools in your relational arsenal, you might soon find yourselves back where you started.

This question is crucial because it directly addresses the practical ability to manage the problems that led to the breakup in the first place. It's not enough to recognize the problems; you need to have the skills to address them effectively.

Consider what new tools you've acquired during the period of separation. Perhaps you've learned assertive communication techniques, or you've developed greater emotional awareness. Maybe you've worked on your self-esteem or learned to better manage anxiety.

Similarly, try to understand if and how your ex has worked on themselves. Have they undergone therapy? Have they read books or attended self-improvement workshops? Have they shown greater openness or willingness to change?

It's important to be realistic about your current capabilities. If neither of you has acquired new tools or skills, you're likely to soon find yourselves reliving the same conflicts and problems. In this case, it might be wise to consider seeking professional help, such as couple's therapy, before committing to the relationship again.

These questions aren't easy to face. They might evoke intense emotions, bring out insecurities. But it's precisely in this vulnerability that strength lies. Addressing them honestly allows you to make a conscious decision, not driven by fear or habit.

The process of answering these questions can be illuminating, but also emotionally demanding. You might discover truths about yourself and the relationship that are difficult to accept. It's important to approach this process with kindness towards yourself, recognizing that personal growth is often accompanied by discomfort.

Consider writing down your answers to these questions. Writing can help you organize your thoughts and see things from a clearer perspective. It can also serve as a future reference, helping you track your progress and remember your insights in moments of doubt.

Remember, there's no right or wrong answer. The goal isn't to discourage reconciliation, but to ensure that if it happens, it's based on solid foundations. That it's a choice, not a reaction.

Self-Assessment and Personal Growth During Relationship Breaks

The end of a relationship can feel like a dark abyss, but it hides an immense transformative potential. It's in these moments of apparent emptiness that we often find the keys to profound personal growth.

Imagine standing in front of a mirror after a breakup. What do you see? Beyond the pain in your eyes, beyond the worry lines, there's a unique opportunity to reinvent yourself, to rediscover parts of you that you may have neglected or forgotten.

The first step in this journey of self-assessment is recognizing that a relationship break isn't just a waiting period. It's precious time for introspection and growth. Start by asking yourself fundamental questions: Who am I outside of this relationship? What are my values, my dreams, my passions?

Often, in relationships, especially those characterized by anxious attachment, we tend to lose parts of ourselves. We adapt, we bend, sometimes we erase ourselves for fear of losing the other. This is the time to reclaim those parts.

Explore new interests or rediscover old passions. Maybe there was a hobby you abandoned, a book you wanted to read, a trip you wished to take. Now is the time. Every new experience is a brick in building your new self.

Personal growth isn't just about acquiring new skills or interests. It's also a process of emotional healing and understanding. Consider keeping an emotional journal. Write down your thoughts, your fears, your hopes. Observe the emotional patterns that emerge. Are there recurring triggers? Reactions that surprise you?

A crucial aspect of this process is learning to manage separation anxiety. For those with anxious attachment, loneliness can seem unbearable. But it's in facing this fear that you find the key to greater emotional security. Try mindfulness techniques or meditation. Learn to be with yourself, to find comfort in your own company.

Remember, personal growth isn't a linear process. There will be days when you feel invincible, others when the desire to return to old habits will be strong. Accept these fluctuations as a natural part of the process.

Another fundamental aspect is building a support network. Cultivate friendships, join support groups, consider therapy. Surrounding yourself with people who support you in your growth journey can make a huge difference.

Finally, use this time to reflect on your expectations in relationships. What have you learned from this experience? What are your real needs in a relationship? How can you communicate them more effectively in the future?

Remember, the goal of this period isn't to become a "perfect" person or immune to pain. It's rather to develop a more authentic and resilient version of yourself. A version that, regardless of whether you decide to reconcile or not, will be better equipped to face future challenges and build healthier, more fulfilling relationships.

Building a Fulfilling Life Outside of Relationships

Have you ever thought that your happiness depended entirely on your partner? It's a common thought, especially for those with anxious attachment. But the truth is, the key to healthy and satisfying relationships lies in cultivating a rich and fulfilling life outside of them.

Imagine your life as a lush garden. A relationship can be a beautiful flower in that garden, but it shouldn't be the only plant. There are many other elements that can make it thrive: friendships, passions, personal goals, professional growth.

The first step is recognizing that you are a complete person, even without a romantic partner. This doesn't mean denying the desire for a relationship, but rather understanding that your worth doesn't depend on your relationship status.

Start by exploring your interests. Is there something you've always wanted to learn? A hobby you've neglected? Now is the perfect time to dedicate yourself to these activities. Not only will they bring you joy and satisfaction, but they'll also help you develop a stronger sense of personal identity.

Friendships are another fundamental pillar of a fulfilling life. Often, when we're in a relationship, we tend to neglect other connections. Reconnect with old friends or make an effort to create new ones. Join clubs, groups, or classes that align with your interests. These connections will not only enrich your life but also provide you with a diversified support system.

Professional growth is another important aspect. Whether you're satisfied with your current job or not, there's always room for learning and development. You might consider taking a course, learning a new skill, or exploring a career change. Having personal goals and ambitions gives you a sense of purpose that goes beyond romantic relationships.

Physical and mental well-being should be a priority. Establish an exercise routine, explore mindfulness or meditation practices, make sure you eat well and get enough sleep. Taking care of yourself isn't selfish; it's a necessity.

An often overlooked aspect is the importance of learning to enjoy your own company. Challenge yourself to do things alone that you would normally do with a partner: go to the movies, dine out, take a trip. It might feel uncomfortable at first, but over time you'll discover a new freedom and self-confidence.

Remember, the goal isn't to fill every moment of your day to avoid thinking about past or future relationships. It's about creating a life that is inherently satisfying, regardless of your relationship status.

As you build this fulfilling life, you might notice a shift in your perspective on relationships. Instead of seeing a partner as someone who "completes" your life, you'll start to see them as someone who further enriches it. This change in perspective is powerful: it allows you to enter relationships from a position of strength and choice, rather than necessity or fear.

Strategies for a Mindful New Beginning

Starting over, whether with an ex or someone new, requires more than just a desire for connection. It demands awareness, intention, and a clear action plan. Here are some key strategies to navigate this delicate terrain with greater confidence and wisdom.

1. Communicate Your Expectations Openly Before diving into a new relationship or reconciling with an ex, clarify to yourself and your partner what you expect. What are your needs? Your boundaries? Your hopes for the future? Open and honest communication from the start can prevent many future misunderstandings.

2. Establish Healthy Boundaries Boundaries aren't walls; they're bridges that allow for safe connection. Clearly define what's acceptable to you and what isn't. This might include the time

you spend together, frequency of communication, or how you handle conflicts. Remember, setting boundaries is an act of self-respect and respect for the other.

3. Practice Emotional Awareness Learn to recognize and manage your emotions, especially those related to attachment anxiety. When you feel overwhelmed, take a step back. Breathe deeply. Ask yourself: "Is this reaction proportionate to the current situation, or am I reacting to old wounds?"

4. Cultivate Independence Maintain your identity and interests outside the relationship. Continue to cultivate friendships, hobbies, and personal goals. A healthy relationship enriches your life; it doesn't completely define it.

5. Address Past Issues If you're starting over with an ex, it's essential to address the problems that led to the previous breakup. Don't expect them to magically disappear. Discuss them openly and create an action plan to handle them differently this time.

6. Be Patient with the Process Change takes time. Don't expect everything to be perfect immediately. There will be ups and downs, moments of doubt and joy. The important thing is to remain committed to the process of growth and learning.

7. Practice Self-Compassion Be kind to yourself during this journey. Making mistakes is human and part of the learning process. Instead of harshly criticizing yourself, ask: "How would I treat a dear friend in this situation?"

8. Seek External Support Don't hesitate to seek professional help if you feel you need it. A therapist or counselor can provide valuable tools and perspectives for navigating the challenges of a new beginning.

9. Maintain a Growth Mindset See every challenge as an opportunity for learning and growth. Instead of viewing problems as insurmountable obstacles, ask yourself: "What can I learn from this situation?"

10. Celebrate Small Progress Recognize and celebrate small steps forward. Every time you handle a situation in a healthier way or feel more secure, take a moment to appreciate how much you've grown.

Remember, a mindful new beginning doesn't guarantee a perfect relationship, but it offers a solid foundation for a more authentic and satisfying connection. With patience, commitment, and a good dose of self-reflection, you can transform your past experiences into wisdom for the future, creating relationships that truly reflect who you are and who you want to become.

Chapter 10:
The Five Key Qualities for Greater Resilience

Have you ever noticed how some people seem to navigate the emotional storms of life with enviable calm, while others feel overwhelmed at the slightest sign of stress? The difference often lies in the ability to tolerate emotional discomfort, a crucial skill for psychological well-being and for building healthy, lasting relationships.

But what does "tolerating emotional discomfort" really mean? Imagine yourself in the middle of a heated argument with your partner. Your heart is racing, your hands are slightly trembling, and you feel an overwhelming urge to raise your voice or leave the room. The ability to tolerate emotional discomfort is what allows you to stay present, truly listen to the other person, and respond thoughtfully instead of reacting impulsively.

This skill is not an innate trait you're born with, but a competence that can be developed and refined over time. Just like a muscle strengthens with exercise, our emotional resilience grows when we allow ourselves to face uncomfortable situations rather than avoid them.

In this chapter, we will explore the five key qualities that form the foundation of this important ability. These qualities not only help us better manage moments of tension in our relationships, but also enable us to live a more authentic and fulfilling life.

Have you ever wondered how your life would be if you could face emotional challenges with greater serenity? What would change in your relationships if you could remain centered even during moments of conflict? As we embark on this journey of discovery, I invite you to reflect on how these qualities manifest in your life and how you could further cultivate them.

Prepare to challenge some of your beliefs, explore new ways of thinking, and most importantly, embark on a path of personal growth that can profoundly transform the way you experience your relationships and your life.

1. A Strong and Pervasive Sense of Self

Think about the last time you truly felt confident in yourself. Perhaps it was during a presentation at work or in an intimate moment with a loved one. That feeling of inner solidity, of knowing exactly who you are and what you want, is at the heart of a strong sense of self.

But what happens when this solidity is put to the test? Imagine finding yourself in the midst of a heated debate with your partner. Emotions are running high, and words are flying. It is in moments like these that a strong sense of self becomes your lifeline.

This is not about stubbornness or inflexibility. On the contrary, it is the ability to stay centered even when everything around you seems in turmoil. It's like having an internal compass that guides you through the turbulent waters of relationships and emotions.

Cultivating this quality takes time and practice. Start by dedicating a few minutes each day to introspection. What truly excites you? What are your core values? These are not questions to answer once and for all but rather an ongoing dialogue with yourself.

As you develop this awareness, you will notice changes in your interactions. You will no longer desperately seek the approval of others because you will already have a deep sense of your own worth. This will allow you to express your needs clearly and establish healthy boundaries in your relationships.

2. Emotional Regulation

Have you ever felt as if your emotions were a wild horse, ready to drag you away at the slightest provocation? Emotional regulation is like learning to tame that horse—not to suppress it, but to ride it with grace.

Think of a moment when you felt overwhelmed by anger or sadness. How did you react? Many of us tend toward two extremes: either we explode, letting the emotion take over, or we try to suppress it completely. Emotional regulation offers a third way.

It's about developing an internal "emotional thermostat." Not to eliminate emotions—they are a vital part of our human experience— but to modulate them. It's the difference between being swept away by the current and knowing how to swim with it.

How can this ability be developed? Awareness is the first step. Start paying attention to your emotions as they arise. Name them without judgment. "I am feeling angry," "I am feeling disappointed." This simple act of labeling can create a breathing space between you and the emotion.

Mindfulness practice can be a powerful ally. Dedicate a few minutes each day to observing your breath and the sensations in your body. Over time, you'll notice that you can observe your emotions without being completely overwhelmed by them.

3. Humility

Humility might seem out of place in a discussion about emotional strength. Yet, it is precisely this quality that often makes the difference between a relationship that grows through difficulties and one that breaks under their weight.

Think about the last time you had to admit you were wrong in an important relationship. How did you feel? Vulnerable, maybe a bit scared? Yet, those moments of honesty and openness are often what truly strengthen a bond.

Humility does not mean belittling yourself or thinking you are less valuable than others. Rather, it is the ability to see yourself and others realistically and compassionately. It is recognizing that all of us, including ourselves, are imperfect human beings, capable of both greatness and mistakes.

This quality allows us to face conflicts and difficulties in relationships with an open mind. Instead of stubbornly clinging to our opinions or trying to "win" at all costs, humility invites us to consider different perspectives and learn from others.

How can humility be cultivated? Start by practicing active listening. The next time you are in a conversation, especially if it is emotionally charged, make a genuine effort to understand the other person's point of view. Don't immediately think about how to respond or counter. Be willing to say, "I don't know" or "I might be wrong."

Humility fosters an environment where mutual respect and growth can thrive, ultimately leading to deeper and more meaningful relationships.

4. Responsibility

Imagine being in the midst of a conflict with a partner or a friend. It's easy to point fingers and see only the faults of the other person. But what if, instead, we took a step back and asked ourselves, "What is my role in this situation?"

Responsibility is like a beacon in the fog of our emotional relationships. It's not about taking all the blame or denying the actions of others. Rather, it's about recognizing that we always have a choice in how we respond to situations, even when we cannot control external circumstances.

This awareness empowers us. Instead of feeling like victims of our emotions or the actions of others, we can take control of our emotional experience. We can choose how to interpret events, how to respond, and how to move toward resolution.

Try paying attention to your inner dialogue. When you find yourself in a difficult situation, notice if you tend to blame others or the circumstances. Then, try shifting your perspective. Ask yourself, "What can I learn from this situation? How can I respond constructively?"

By adopting this mindset, you can navigate conflicts more effectively, leading to personal growth and healthier, more resilient relationships.

5. Healthy Self-Esteem

Healthy self-esteem is like fertile soil on which all the other qualities we've discussed can grow. But what does it really mean? It's not about believing you are perfect or superior to others. Instead, it is a deep acceptance of yourself, with all your strengths and weaknesses.

Think of a time when you faced a difficult challenge. How did you talk to yourself? People with healthy self-esteem are capable of self-encouragement. They don't get discouraged in the face of difficulties but approach them with compassion and determination.

This quality allows us to better tolerate emotional discomfort because we don't see every criticism or disagreement as a threat to our identity. We can remain open to feedback and different perspectives without feeling diminished.

How can healthy self-esteem be cultivated? Start by practicing self-compassion. Treat yourself with the same kindness you would offer a dear friend. Recognize that mistakes and imperfections are part of the human experience and do not diminish your worth.

Challenging negative thoughts is another powerful practice. When you catch yourself being overly critical, stop and ask, "Is this really true? How would I speak to a friend in this situation?"

Developing these five qualities is a journey, not a destination. There will be moments of progress and moments of challenge. But with patience and practice, you can build a solid foundation to face emotional discomfort with greater resilience and grace.

Challenges in Environment and Implementation

Developing the ability to tolerate emotional discomfort is not a journey without obstacles. Often, the world around us seems to conspire against our efforts for personal growth. Take social media, for example: a constant stream of comparisons, opinions, and judgments that can undermine even the most solid self-esteem.

Think about the last time you scrolled through your feed. How many times did you find yourself comparing your life to the seemingly perfect lives of others? This tendency for constant comparison can make it difficult to maintain a stable sense of self and healthy self-esteem.

But the challenges aren't limited to the digital world. In our daily interactions, we can also encounter resistance when we try to implement these new skills. Imagine finding yourself in a heated discussion with a colleague. You are trying to apply the emotional regulation techniques you've learned, but your counterpart keeps provoking you. In such situations, staying calm can seem almost impossible.

And what about social expectations? In many cultures, the open expression of emotions is viewed with suspicion, especially for men. This can make it difficult to practice the humility and vulnerability necessary for true emotional growth.

Despite these challenges, it's important to remember that every step forward, no matter how small, is a success. The key is to stay aware of your progress, celebrating small victories along the way. Perhaps today you managed to stay calm in a situation that would have made you explode in the past. Or maybe you had the courage to express a vulnerable emotion to a friend. These are all significant steps towards greater emotional resilience.

The journey toward greater tolerance of emotional discomfort is a personal one, influenced by multiple factors. But with patience, practice, and a good dose of self-compassion, it is possible to overcome these challenges and build deeper, more satisfying relationships.

Impact on the Quality of Relationships

Cultivating the ability to tolerate emotional discomfort is not just an exercise in personal growth; it has a profound and transformative impact on our relationships. Imagine how your life would change if you could face conflicts with calm and presence, instead of reacting impulsively.

Relationships, whether romantic, familial, or friendly, often serve as the testing ground for our emotional skills. It's easy to be patient and understanding when everything is going well, but true strength in a bond emerges during times of tension.

Picture yourself in the midst of an argument with your partner. In the past, you might have raised your voice, said things you later regretted, or completely shut down. But now, thanks to your practice of emotional tolerance, you manage to stay present. You truly listen without jumping to conclusions. You express your feelings honestly without blaming. This shift can completely transform the dynamics of your relationship.

The ability to tolerate emotional discomfort also allows us to be more authentic in our interactions. We no longer feel the need to hide parts of ourselves out of fear of judgment. This authenticity naturally attracts deeper and more meaningful relationships.

Moreover, when we can manage our emotions healthily, we become a safe harbor for others. Our friends and family feel more comfortable sharing their vulnerabilities with us, knowing that we can offer stable support.

It's not about becoming stoic or never experiencing negative emotions. On the contrary, it is the ability to navigate the full range of human emotions without being overwhelmed that enriches our relationships. This emotional resilience allows us to stay connected even in difficult times, creating bonds that can withstand the storms of life.

By facing conflicts with composure and empathy, we build trust and mutual respect, fostering an environment where both parties can grow and flourish. This not only strengthens the relationship but also enhances our overall well-being, as we experience the profound satisfaction of deep, supportive connections.

Chapter 11:
The Four Phases That Transform Your Attachment

Have you ever thought about learning a new skill and felt overwhelmed by the idea of not even knowing where to start? Or perhaps you've embarked on a personal growth journey and wondered why it sometimes seems so difficult to see progress? The Conscious Competence Model offers an enlightening answer to these questions, providing a valuable map for our journey of learning and growth.

Imagine standing before a mountain that represents your personal challenge, whether it's improving your relationships, developing new professional skills, or working on your emotional security. The Conscious Competence Model is like a compass guiding you through four distinct phases of this journey, each with its unique challenges and revelations.

This model isn't just an abstract theory confined to academic classrooms. It's a practical and powerful tool that can transform the way you approach any new learning in your life. Whether you're looking to enhance your relationships, learn a new language, or overcome your deepest fears, this model offers a perspective that can radically change your approach.

But where does this revolutionary model come from? Its origin is shrouded in a fascinating attribution mystery. Some attribute it to Martin M. Broadwell, who described the four levels of teaching in 1969. Others cite the work of Paul Curtis and Philip Warren, who discussed it in their 1973 book on life skills coaching dynamics. Still, others credit its development to Noel Burch in the 1970s at Gordon Training International.

Regardless of its precise origins, the Conscious Competence Model has proven its value in a wide range of fields, from education to business to psychology. And now we're about to explore how this model can illuminate the path to healing from anxious attachment.

In the upcoming sections, we'll delve into each of the four phases of the model in detail. You'll see how these phases manifest in the healing process of attachment and discover practical strategies for navigating each one.

Prepare for a journey of discovery that could change not only how you view your growth path but also how you tackle every new challenge in your life. Are you ready to explore the depths of your awareness and unlock potentials you may not have even known you had?

Phase 1: Unconscious Incompetence

Have you ever found yourself in a situation where you thought you had everything under control, only to later discover how unprepared you actually were? Welcome to the phase of unconscious incompetence, the starting point of our journey through the Conscious Competence Model.

In this phase, not only do we not know how to do something, but we are also unaware of our lack of knowledge or skills. It's like being in a dark room without knowing there is a light switch. We not only can't see, but we don't even know there is something to see.

In the context of attachment healing, this phase is particularly insidious. Imagine constantly finding yourself in problematic relationships without realizing that your anxious attachment style is deeply influencing your interactions. You might think, "I'm just unlucky in love," or "All my partners are emotionally distant," without realizing that your behavior might be contributing to these recurring patterns.

During this phase, it's common to project your problems onto others. You might focus solely on your partner's flaws, convinced that if only they changed, everything would be fine. This projection serves as a defense mechanism, protecting you from the painful realization that you might have a role in creating or maintaining problematic relational dynamics.

But how does this phase concretely manifest in the journey of attachment healing? You might find yourself:

- Repeating the same destructive relationship patterns without realizing your role in them.

- Always blaming relational problems on others without ever questioning your own behaviors.

- Overreacting to situations of relational stress without understanding why.

- Constantly seeking reassurance from your partner without realizing how suffocating this behavior can be.

The key to progressing beyond this phase is exposure to new information and perspectives. It might be a book on attachment that comes into your hands, an enlightening conversation with a friend, or a series of experiences that finally make you question your assumptions.

Remember, being in this phase is not a failure or a flaw. It is simply the starting point of your journey towards greater awareness and personal growth. The real challenge lies in staying open to the possibility that there is much more to learn about ourselves and our relationships than we ever imagined.

As you reflect on this phase, ask yourself: are there areas in your relational life where you might be unconsciously incompetent? What signals might you have ignored? And most importantly, are you ready to open your eyes to new possibilities of understanding and growth?

Phase 2: Conscious Incompetence

Have you ever experienced that uncomfortable feeling of suddenly realizing how little you knew about something you thought you understood well? Welcome to the phase of conscious incompetence, a crucial moment in your journey of personal growth and attachment healing.

In this phase, you become painfully aware of what you don't know or can't do. It's as if the light has finally been turned on in that dark room, revealing a mess you didn't know existed. This new awareness can be both enlightening and discouraging.

In the context of attachment healing, this phase often begins with a revelation. Perhaps you read a book on anxious attachment and found yourself on every page. Or maybe a therapist pointed out behavioral patterns you were unaware of. Suddenly, you clearly see how your attachment style has influenced your relationships, and this awareness can be overwhelming.

During this phase, you might experience:

- A sense of frustration in recognizing problematic behaviors without yet knowing how to change them.

- Moments of intense self-criticism when you realize how your attachment style has negatively impacted past relationships.

- A sudden awareness of your excessive emotional reactions, even if you can't yet control them.

- A desire to change, accompanied by the feeling of not knowing where to start.

This phase can be emotionally challenging. You might feel overwhelmed by the amount of work ahead of you or discouraged by the perceived distance between where you are and where you want to be. It's important to remember that these feelings are normal and are actually signs of progress.

The key to navigating this phase is patience and self-compassion. Remember, awareness is the first step toward change. Even if you don't yet have all the tools to modify your behaviors, simply being aware is a huge step forward.

This is also the phase where observation becomes crucial. Start noticing your behavioral patterns without judging them. When you find yourself in a situation that triggers your attachment anxieties, mentally step back and observe your reactions. What do you feel in your body? What thoughts cross your mind? This type of mindful awareness is the foundation upon which you will build your future competencies.

Remember, conscious incompetence can be uncomfortable, but it is also incredibly fertile. It is the ground from which new understandings and skills will grow. Embrace this phase with curiosity and openness, knowing that every moment of awareness brings you one step closer to healing.

As you reflect on this phase, ask yourself: In what areas of your relational life do you currently feel incompetent but aware? How can you use this awareness as a springboard for change? And most importantly, how can you be kind to yourself as you navigate these uncharted waters of personal growth?

Phase 3: Conscious Competence

Do you remember the first time you drove a car? You were probably focused on every single movement: shifting gears, checking mirrors, pressing the pedals at the right moment. This is the essence of conscious competence, the third phase of our journey through the Conscious Competence Model.

In this phase, you finally start to see the fruits of your hard work. You've acquired new skills and can put them into practice, but doing so still requires conscious concentration and deliberate effort. It's like learning to dance: you know the steps, but you still need to count them in your head.

In the context of attachment healing, this phase manifests in powerful and transformative ways:

- Recognizing Emotional Triggers: You begin to recognize your emotional triggers before they escalate, allowing you to respond more calmly.

- Communicating Needs Clearly: You can communicate your needs more clearly and assertively, even though it still requires conscious effort.

- Practicing Emotional Self-Regulation: You manage to practice emotional self-regulation when feeling anxious, using techniques like deep breathing or mindfulness.

- Questioning Anxious Thoughts: You can challenge your anxious thoughts and consider alternative perspectives, even though this process still requires active engagement.

This phase can be both rewarding and frustrating. On one hand, you clearly see your progress, which can be incredibly motivating. On the other hand, you might feel frustrated by the constant effort required to implement these new skills.

It's crucial in this phase to celebrate every small success. Did you handle a difficult conversation without being overwhelmed by anxiety? Did you resist the urge to seek excessive reassurance? These are all notable triumphs in your healing journey.

At the same time, it's important to be patient with yourself. Learning new emotional and relational skills takes time and practice. There will be moments when you fall back into old patterns, and that's okay. The important thing is to recognize these moments as learning opportunities rather than failures.

An essential aspect of this phase is constant practice. The more you implement your new skills, the more natural they will become. You might find it helpful to keep a journal of your interactions, noting when you successfully applied your new skills and how you felt doing so.

Remember, conscious competence is a bridge between learning and mastery. Every time you consciously practice a new skill, you are building stronger neural connections, making that competence an increasingly integral part of you.

As you reflect on this phase, ask yourself: What new skills are you actively practicing in your attachment healing journey? How can you create more opportunities to practice these skills in your daily life? And how can you be kinder to yourself during this process of learning and growth?

Phase 4: Unconscious Competence

Unconscious competence represents the pinnacle of the attachment healing journey. It is the moment when new skills and healthy behaviors become second nature, flowing effortlessly without conscious effort.

Imagine dancing with your partner. At first, you counted every step, focusing on each movement. Now, you move gracefully, perfectly synchronized, without thinking about the steps. The music guides your movements, and you respond instinctively. This is what happens when you reach unconscious competence in your attachment style.

The manifestations of this phase are subtle but profound. Communicating your needs becomes natural and assertive, without the anxiety or hesitation that previously accompanied it. Boundaries in relationships are established and maintained effortlessly, without the burden of guilt. Trust, both in yourself and in your partner, is deeply rooted, eliminating the constant need for reassurance.

Conflicts, once a source of panic, transform into opportunities for growth. You approach them with calmness and openness, seeing them as a natural aspect of relationships rather than threats. This new perspective arises from the inner security you have developed.

However, unconscious competence is not without its challenges. Paradoxically, the very ease with which you now navigate your relationships can lead to a kind of complacency. It is crucial to maintain an attitude of openness and humility, recognizing that personal growth is an endless journey.

Additionally, you might find it difficult to articulate how you do what you do. Your actions and reactions, now so natural, can seem mysterious to those still struggling with their own insecure attachment. This can be challenging if you wish to help others on their healing journey.

Unconscious competence does not mean perfection or the absence of difficult moments. What changes is your ability to face these challenges with resilience and grace. Insecurities may still emerge, but they no longer destabilize you as they once did.

As you navigate this new reality of secure attachment, you may discover new areas for growth. Life continues to present challenges and learning opportunities. The difference is that you now face these new experiences from a foundation of security and self-trust.

Reflecting on how you have arrived at this point can be powerful. Think back on your journey, the challenges you have overcome, and the insights you have gained. This reflection not only reinforces your new reality but can also inspire you to continue your growth in other areas of your life.

As you move forward, consider these questions: What new areas of growth are emerging for you? How can you maintain your humility and openness to learning? And how can you use your journey to inspire and guide others who are still on their path to healing?

Applying the Model to the Attachment Healing Process

The journey of attachment healing is unique for each individual, but the Conscious Competence Model offers a valuable map for navigating this path. Let's see how each phase specifically manifests in the context of healing anxious attachment.

In unconscious incompetence, a person with anxious attachment might repeatedly engage in destructive relational patterns without realizing their role in them. They might seek emotionally unavailable partners, believing that love must be a constant struggle. Projection of problems onto others is common in this phase, with the belief that "if only my partner changed, everything would be fine."

The transition to conscious incompetence often occurs through a series of failed relationships or a sudden realization, perhaps triggered by reading or therapy. Suddenly, the person recognizes their anxious behaviors—constantly seeking reassurance, fearing abandonment, tending to smother their partner—but still doesn't know how to change them.

The phase of conscious competence is where the real healing work begins. The person actively learns and applies new strategies to manage their anxiety. They might practice mindfulness to calm anxious thoughts, use assertive communication techniques to express their needs, or work on self-esteem to reduce emotional dependency. These new behaviors require conscious effort and constant practice.

Finally, in unconscious competence, the new skills become second nature. The person no longer has to consciously think about how to react in situations that previously triggered anxiety. They maintain healthy relationships with ease, communicate their needs without fear, and handle conflicts with calm and confidence.

It's important to note that this process is not linear. There may be moments of regression, especially in highly stressful situations.

However, each "relapse" offers an opportunity for further learning and growth.

Applying this model to attachment healing highlights the importance of patience and perseverance. Change takes time, and each phase of the process is crucial. Recognizing which phase you are in can provide valuable perspective and help maintain motivation during the healing journey.

Additionally, this model underscores the importance of external support. A therapist, coach, or support group can provide the necessary guidance to progress through these phases, offering tools, feedback, and encouragement along the way.

The awareness gained through this process is not limited to romantic relationships. Often, people find that healing their anxious attachment has a positive ripple effect on all aspects of their lives, from friendships to family relationships, to the professional sphere.

Chapter 12:
Healing Strategies for Anxious Attachment

Have you ever wondered why you always seem to know what others want, but can't figure out what you desire? Welcome to the world of "outside-in orientation," a behavioral pattern that many people with anxious attachment develop from childhood.

Imagine being a child in an unpredictable environment, where your parents' love and attention depend on their mood at the moment. How do you survive? You develop an almost supernatural ability to read others' emotions. You become an expert in understanding what others want, even before they know it themselves.

This childhood survival strategy turns into a way of living. You grow up continuing to put others first, ignoring your own needs and desires. You find yourself an adult, still constantly seeking external approval, as if your existence depends on others' judgments.

But what is the cost of this behavior? Unbalanced relationships, where you give too much and receive too little. A constant feeling of inner emptiness because you don't really know who you are beyond others' expectations. Chronic anxiety stemming from the impossible task of controlling how others perceive you.

It's time to change perspective. To turn your gaze inward. Here are some practical steps to start this journey of rediscovery:

1. Practice inner listening. Spend a few minutes each day asking yourself: "What do I really want? How do I feel?" without judging the answers.

2. Keep an emotion journal. Note how you feel in different situations, without seeking anyone's approval.

3. Learn to say no. Start with small things. Decline an invitation if you don't feel like going out. Express a different opinion in a casual conversation.

4. Cultivate your interests. Spend time on hobbies and activities you are passionate about, regardless of what others think.

Remember, change takes time and practice. There will be moments when you fall back into old patterns. But every step towards rediscovering yourself is a victory. You are laying the foundation for more balanced and satisfying relationships, and most importantly, for a more authentic and fulfilling life.

Next time you catch yourself obsessively seeking others' approval, stop. Take a deep breath and ask yourself: "What do I want?" The answer might surprise you.

Master Your Feelings

Emotions overwhelm you like a sudden wave. Your heart races, your hands tremble, and your mind fills with chaotic thoughts. You feel overwhelmed, unable to control this inner storm. Welcome to the world of anxious attachment, where emotions seem to have the power to completely dominate you.

But what if you could learn to ride these emotional waves instead of being swept away by them? What if you could turn this sensitivity into a strength rather than a weakness?

Think of your emotions as a constantly moving sea. Sometimes calm, other times stirred by powerful waves. The goal is not to eliminate the waves—they are an integral part of the sea, just as emotions are part of your human experience. The secret lies in learning to navigate them skillfully.

The first step is awareness. Start noticing your emotions without judging them. Observe how they manifest in your body. Maybe anger is a heat rising to your face, anxiety a knot in your stomach, sadness a weight on your chest. This detached observation is like watching the waves from above: it allows you to see them without being immediately overwhelmed.

Once you've developed this awareness, you can begin to explore techniques to regulate the intensity of your emotions. Deep breathing, for example, is like an anchor that keeps you steady even in the most turbulent waters. Try this: inhale slowly while counting to four, hold your breath for four seconds, then exhale for four. Repeat this cycle a few times and notice how your body starts to calm down.

But true emotional mastery goes beyond mere calmness. It involves understanding the message behind each emotion. The fear of abandonment, so common in anxious attachment, might actually be a signal of your need for connection and security. Instead of being paralyzed by this fear, use it as motivation to cultivate deeper and more authentic relationships.

Learn to communicate your emotions clearly and non-accusatorily. Instead of saying, "You make me angry when you don't reply to my messages," try, "I feel anxious when I don't get a response because I fear I'm not important to you." This approach opens the door to dialogue instead of closing it with an accusation.

Remember, mastering your emotions doesn't mean suppressing or ignoring them. It's about embracing them, understanding them, and using them as a compass to navigate the complexities of human relationships. With practice and patience, you'll find that those same waves that once terrified you can now carry you to new and exciting emotional destinations.

As you learn to ride your emotional waves, you'll notice a profound change not only in yourself but also in your relationships. Your new emotional stability will create a positive ripple effect, influencing those around you. And with this newfound mastery, you'll be ready to explore new horizons, both emotional and relational.

Transformative Goals

Have you ever wondered what your life would be like if you weren't constantly worried about relationships? If the anxiety of abandonment didn't hold you back from pursuing your dreams? It's time to explore a new territory: your personal desires and ambitions.

Anxious attachment often traps us in an invisible cage. We focus so much on maintaining relationships that we forget to cultivate ourselves. But what if we started to see personal growth as the key to healthier, more fulfilling relationships?

Think about a skill you've always wanted to develop. Maybe it's learning a new language, playing an instrument, or even starting your own business. Now, imagine dedicating the same energy to this goal that you usually invest in trying to control your relationships. Intimidating, right? But also incredibly liberating.

Start with small steps. Choose a goal that excites you but doesn't overwhelm you. It could be something simple like reading a book a week or taking a 30-minute walk every day. The important thing is that it's something you do for yourself, not to please others.

As you achieve these small milestones, you'll notice a subtle but profound change. Your self-esteem will grow, no longer based solely on others' approval, but on a sense of personal accomplishment. This new sense of value will make you paradoxically more attractive in your relationships, creating a virtuous cycle of growth and connection.

Don't be afraid to dream big. That trip you've always postponed? Plan it. That career that seemed out of reach? Take the first step. Every time you push beyond your limits, you're rewriting the narrative of your life.

Remember, the goal is not to become so independent that you don't need others. It's about creating a healthy balance between independence and connection. As you pursue your goals, you may find your relationships evolving naturally. You'll attract people who appreciate your growth and support your journey.

And when the anxiety of abandonment surfaces—because it will—use your new emotional awareness skills to recognize and manage it. Remember that you are building a rich and fulfilling life, one that doesn't depend solely on others for your happiness.

Expanding your horizons doesn't mean abandoning your relationships. On the contrary, it means enriching them with new experiences, perspectives, and a more complete version of yourself. Every new goal you achieve is a step towards a more balanced and satisfying life, where relationships are a precious part, but not the only source of meaning and joy.

As you venture into this new territory of personal growth, keep in mind that the journey is as important as the destination. Celebrate each step forward, learn from moments of difficulty, and most importantly, enjoy the process of discovering who you truly are beyond your attachments.

Connect Authentically

Have you ever felt that your words fail to truly express what you feel inside? As if there's a chasm between what you want to say and what actually comes out of your mouth? For those living with anxious attachment, communication can often feel like a minefield, full of potential misunderstandings and hidden fears.

Imagine being able to express your deepest thoughts and feelings without the constant fear of being judged or abandoned. Does it seem like an unattainable dream? It's not. The key lies in learning to communicate from the heart, in an authentic and vulnerable way.

The first step towards deeper communication is self-awareness. Before expressing your feelings to others, you need to be able to recognize and accept them yourself. Take a moment to reflect: what are you truly feeling in this moment? Fear? Anger? Joy? Accept these emotions without judging them.

Now, instead of hiding these emotions or expressing them indirectly, try to communicate them openly. Use phrases that start with "I feel" or "I experience," focusing on your personal experience rather than accusing or blaming others. For example, instead of saying "You are neglecting me," you might say "I feel neglected and need more attention."

Vulnerability is the key to deeper connections. Yes, it can be scary to open up and show your insecurities. But it is this very authenticity that allows others to truly see you and connect with you on a deeper level.

Remember, communication is a two-way process. As you learn to express yourself more authentically, also practice the art of active listening. Listen not only to the other person's words but also to the tone of voice and body language. Try to understand not just what the other person is saying, but also what they are feeling.

A powerful exercise is to practice non-verbal communication. Sit across from a trusted friend and spend a few minutes looking into each other's eyes without speaking. What do you notice? What do you feel? This exercise might seem awkward at first, but it can teach you a lot about communication that goes beyond words.

As you practice this form of more authentic communication, you might notice that your relationships start to change. Conversations become deeper, connections more meaningful. You might find that people in your life appreciate your new honesty and openness.

Remember, authentic communication doesn't guarantee that others will always respond the way you hope. There will still be moments of misunderstanding or disappointment. But you will have the satisfaction of knowing that you are expressing yourself in a true and sincere way.

As you continue this journey towards more authentic communication, be patient with yourself. It will take time and practice to overcome old patterns and fears. Celebrate every small progress, every conversation where you felt truly heard and understood.

True connection begins with being authentic with yourself. When you learn to communicate from the depths of your being, you open the door to richer, more fulfilling, and more genuine relationships. And in this process, you might discover parts of yourself that you didn't even know existed.

Love Yourself

Self-love is not selfishness. It is the fertile ground on which authentic and fulfilling relationships grow. Yet, for those who have lived with anxious attachment, this concept can seem alien, almost dangerous.

Think of self-love as a daily practice, not a goal to achieve. Start with small acts of kindness toward yourself. Maybe it's taking five minutes of silence in the morning or preparing your favorite meal even if you're alone. These seemingly insignificant gestures send a powerful message to your subconscious: you are worthy of care and attention.

The real breakthrough comes when you start treating yourself with the same compassion you would reserve for a dear friend. Observe your inner dialogue. Often, we are our own harshest critics, ready to flog ourselves for the slightest mistake. Instead, try speaking to yourself with kindness. When you make a mistake, instead of self-flagellation, ask yourself: "What can I learn from this experience?"

This new relationship with yourself inevitably reflects in your external relationships. When you learn to value yourself, you stop desperately seeking validation from others. Your interactions become more authentic, less burdened by unrealistic expectations.

Self-care goes beyond mere pampering. It also means setting healthy boundaries, saying no when necessary, and taking responsibility for your own emotional well-being. It's no longer the job of your partner or friends to "save" or "complete" you. You are already whole.

As you cultivate this new relationship with yourself, you might notice surprising changes in your interpersonal dynamics. People respond differently to those who have a sense of intrinsic worth. You attract relationships based on mutual respect rather than emotional dependency.

Remember, self-love is not a destination but an ongoing journey. There will be days when it feels easier and days when it seems impossible. What matters is the constant practice, the gentle return to yourself every time you stray.

This path of self-love is perhaps the greatest challenge for those who have lived with anxious attachment. But it is also the most precious gift you can give yourself. Because when you truly learn to love yourself, you discover an inexhaustible source of strength and serenity within you.

And so, as you continue this journey of healing and growth, remember that every step toward self-love is a step toward healthier and more fulfilling relationships. It's not just work on yourself, but an investment in all your future connections.

Chapter 13:

From Anxious to Secure in 10 Steps

Detachment is not indifference. It is freedom. It is the key to moving from anxious to secure attachment, a journey that transforms not only our relationships but our entire way of being in the world.

This journey begins with a realization: our struggles with anxiety in relationships often have deep roots, dating back to childhood. Perhaps there was someone – a parent, a caregiver – whose approval we desperately sought. This search for approval can follow us into adulthood, manifesting as a constant need for validation and a paralyzing fear of abandonment.

But what if we could let go of this need? What if we could free ourselves from the burden of constantly seeking others' approval?

The emotional detachment we seek does not mean becoming cold or insensitive. On the contrary, it means reaching a point where our happiness and worth no longer depend on the actions or opinions of others. It means developing a solid foundation of self-esteem and inner security.

This journey requires courage. It requires the willingness to look honestly within ourselves, to face our deepest fears, and to challenge the behavior patterns that no longer serve us.

In the following sections, we will explore ten crucial steps to mastering the art of detachment. These steps are not easy, but each one is a powerful tool for personal transformation.

Prepare to challenge your beliefs, question your behaviors, and, most importantly, rediscover yourself. Because in the end, true detachment is not about letting go of others, but about finding and fully embracing yourself.

Step 1 - Freeing Yourself from the Need for Approval

The first step toward emotional detachment is recognizing and then freeing yourself from the obsessive need for approval. This need often stems from childhood experiences where love or attention seemed conditional on our behavior.

Imagine spending years trying to earn the affection of someone who, for whatever reason, was unable to give it fully. Perhaps it was an emotionally distant parent or an inconsistent caregiver. This experience creates a pattern: we constantly try to "earn" others' love, as if it were a reward for our actions rather than an unconditional gift.

Real change begins when we realize that we cannot control others' actions or feelings. No matter how hard we try, we cannot force someone to love or approve of us. And more importantly, we shouldn't want to.

Detachment in this context means accepting that a person's intrinsic value does not depend on external approval. It means recognizing that we are worthy of love and respect regardless of what others think of us.

This process of liberation can be painful. It might mean facing old wounds, accepting that some people will never give us what we seek from them. But it is also incredibly liberating.

When we free ourselves from the need for approval, we begin to live more authentically. We no longer shape our behavior to please others, but act in line with our true values and desires. This not only boosts our self-esteem but also attracts more genuine and fulfilling relationships.

Remember, detachment does not mean no longer desiring meaningful connections or relationships. Instead, it means approaching them from a position of inner strength and completeness rather than from a place of lack or desperate need.

The journey to free yourself from the need for approval requires constant practice. Start by observing your thoughts and behaviors. When you catch yourself obsessively seeking someone's approval, stop. Breathe. Remind yourself that your worth does not depend on their opinion.

Gradually, you will discover that true freedom lies not in controlling others' perceptions, but in letting go of the need to control them. And in this freedom, you will find a new strength and inner peace that no external approval can ever provide.

Step 2 - Letting Go of Control Over Others

The second crucial step in the journey toward detachment is learning to let go of the desire to control others. This desire often stems from a deep sense of insecurity and the mistaken belief that we can ensure our emotional safety by manipulating others' actions and feelings.

Reflect on how many times you've tried to "manage" someone's behavior to feel more secure. Perhaps you've obsessively monitored your partner's movements on social media, or tried to dictate who they can or cannot spend time with. These attempts at control are not only ineffective in the long run, but they can also seriously damage your relationships.

True power lies in recognizing that the only person you can truly control is yourself. This means accepting that others have the right to make their own choices, even when those choices might hurt or disappoint you.

Letting go of control does not mean becoming passive or indifferent. On the contrary, it means shifting the focus from trying to control others to working on yourself. Instead of trying to change your partner or your friends, focus on how you can better manage your own emotions and reactions.

This shift in perspective can be initially frightening. It might feel like you're giving up your "security." But in reality, you are gaining something much more valuable: emotional freedom.

When you stop trying to control others, you begin to see people for who they truly are, not for who you want them to be. This leads to more authentic and satisfying relationships. Additionally, by freeing yourself from the burden of trying to manage others, you'll have more energy to dedicate to your personal growth.

Practice the art of "letting go." When you catch yourself wanting to control a situation or a person, take a deep breath and remind yourself that it is not your job to manage others' actions. Instead, focus on how you can respond to the situation in a healthy and constructive way.

Remember, true control is not about shaping the external world to fit your desires, but about cultivating the inner strength to face any situation with grace and resilience. In this way, you will find a security that no external control can ever provide.

Step 3 - Loving Yourself Beyond Performance

The third fundamental step in the journey toward detachment is learning to love yourself regardless of your performance or external achievements. Too often, we confuse our intrinsic value with what we achieve or how others perceive us.

Think about how many times you have based your self-esteem on external factors: a compliment received, a promotion at work, or the attention of someone you like. While these successes can certainly be gratifying, tying your sense of self-worth to them is a recipe for chronic insecurity.

True self-love goes beyond performance. It's about accepting and valuing who you are at your core, independent of what you do or achieve. This kind of self-acceptance is not conditioned by success or failure but remains constant through life's ups and downs.

Start by observing how you talk to yourself. Are you your biggest critic or your biggest supporter? Challenge those negative thoughts that tell you you are only as good as your last achievement. Remind yourself that your worth as a person is not defined by what you do, but by who you are.

Practice kindness toward yourself. Treat yourself with the same compassion and understanding you would offer a dear friend. Celebrate your successes, yes, but don't let them become the measure of your worth.

Develop interests and passions that are not tied to tangible outcomes. Do things simply because you enjoy them, not to impress others or achieve a certain status. This will help you cultivate a sense of joy and satisfaction that comes from within, not from external validation.

Remember that being "lovable" does not mean being perfect. In fact, it is often our imperfections and vulnerabilities that make us unique and interesting. Embrace your quirks and "flaws" as integral parts of who you are.

As you learn to love yourself unconditionally, you will notice a change in your relationships. You will no longer desperately seek others' approval because you already have the most important approval: your own.

This self-love is not selfishness. On the contrary, it is the foundation for healthier and more authentic relationships. When you love and accept yourself for who you truly are, you are able to offer the same unconditional love to others.

The journey to self-love is continuous. There will be days when it is easier and days when it is challenging. What matters is the constant practice and kindness toward yourself along the way.

Step 4 - Authenticity in Long-Term Relationships

The idea of changing yourself to please a partner might seem romantic, almost heroic. But the truth? It's a path that inevitably leads to frustration and resentment. Authenticity, on the other hand, is the key to building lasting and deeply fulfilling relationships.

Think about it: how many times have you found yourself suppressing parts of yourself, hiding your true desires or opinions for fear of creating conflict or being rejected? This behavior, while it may seem like a short-term survival strategy, slowly erodes the very foundation of the relationship.

Authenticity requires courage. It means showing your vulnerabilities, expressing your needs without filters, and sometimes risking rejection. But it is precisely this honesty that creates the space for true intimacy.

Imagine being able to be completely yourself, with all your strengths and flaws, and being loved for exactly that. Isn't that the essence of what we all seek in a relationship?

Being authentic doesn't mean being insensitive or selfish. On the contrary, it means creating a space where both partners can express themselves freely, grow individually and together. It's an invitation for your partner to do the same, to show up as their true self.

This approach may seem risky. And it is. But consider the alternative: a life spent playing a role, stifling parts of yourself for fear of losing the other's love. Isn't that too high a price to pay?

Authenticity in long-term relationships also requires the ability to evolve together. It's not about remaining static but growing while maintaining your essence. It's a delicate balance between staying true to yourself and adapting to life's and your partner's changes.

When we embrace authenticity, we lay the groundwork for deeper, more resilient, and infinitely more rewarding relationships. It's not an easy path, but it's the only one that leads to true connection.

So, as you navigate the sometimes turbulent waters of long-term relationships, remember: your authenticity is not just a gift to yourself, but also to your partner and the relationship itself.

Step 5 - Authentic Connection Instead of Control

The desire for control in relationships often reflects our deepest insecurities. We think that if we can control the other person, we can protect ourselves from pain, rejection, and abandonment. But this is an illusion that deprives us of the true essence of an authentic connection.

Imagine letting go of the reins, allowing the relationship to breathe and evolve naturally. Scary? Perhaps. But it is in this space of freedom that true intimacy blossoms.

Control is a wall we build around ourselves, believing it will protect us. But in reality, it isolates us. It prevents us from experiencing true vulnerability, true connection. When we try to control the other, we are essentially saying: "I don't trust you, I don't trust us."

Authentic connection, on the other hand, is a bridge. It is an invitation to explore together, grow together, fall, and rise together. It's not about forcing the other to conform to our expectations but about creating a space where both can be fully themselves.

This does not mean abandoning all forms of structure or expectation in the relationship. Rather, it means replacing rigid control with a fluid dance of giving and receiving, talking and listening, approaching and distancing.

In practice, this could mean:

- Truly listening without the urgency to fix or change
- Expressing your own needs and desires without demanding that the other always meet them
- Accepting that your partner can have experiences, friendships, and interests outside the relationship
- Facing conflicts as opportunities for growth, not as threats to be suppressed

When we let go of control in favor of authentic connection, we discover a deeper and more fulfilling form of intimacy. It's no longer a power game but a dance of mutual respect and understanding.

So, as you navigate your relationships, ask yourself: are you trying to control or to connect? The answer could open the door to a world of relational possibilities you never imagined.

Step 6 - Responsibility to Yourself

We are born alone and we will die alone. This truth, as bleak as it may seem, actually holds a powerful lesson about personal responsibility. Too often, we try to delegate our happiness, well-being, and even our sense of identity to others. But the reality is that the only person truly responsible for you is yourself.

Think about how many times you've waited for someone else to "complete" you or make you happy. Maybe you've spent years searching for the perfect partner, convinced that once you found them, all your problems would disappear. Or perhaps you've constantly sought approval from your parents, friends, or bosses, hoping their recognition would finally give you the sense of worth you were looking for.

But true freedom, true power, lies in recognizing that you are the architect of your own life. It's not about denying the importance of relationships or support from others. It's about understanding that at the end of the day, you are the one who has to live with yourself.

This shift in perspective can be liberating. Instead of waiting for someone else to solve your problems or fill your voids, you start asking: "What can I do for myself?" You begin to see every challenge, every disappointment, not as a punishment but as an opportunity for growth and self-improvement.

Taking responsibility for yourself also means learning to set healthy boundaries. It means saying no when necessary, even if it might disappoint others. It means taking care of your physical and mental well-being, even when it would be easier to neglect yourself to please others.

Don't misunderstand: taking responsibility for yourself doesn't mean isolating yourself or rejecting help from others. On the contrary, it allows you to enter relationships from a place of strength and authenticity. When you don't rely on others for your happiness or sense of worth, you are free to love and appreciate them for who they are, not for what they can give you.

Remember: you are the only person guaranteed to spend every single moment of your life with. Doesn't it make sense to invest in this relationship, to cultivate it, to nurture it? When you start treating yourself with the same love and respect you desire from others, you discover a source of strength and resilience that no external circumstance can shake.

So, as you face life's challenges, remember: you are the protagonist of your story. Embrace this responsibility, not as a burden, but as your personal superpower.

Step 7 - Self-Acceptance and Embracing Your Heritage

How many times have you looked in the mirror, focusing only on what you wish to change? Perhaps you've spent years trying to conform to unrealistic beauty standards or hiding parts of yourself that you deemed unacceptable.

But what if I told you that every feature of your face, every curve of your body, tells a story that goes far beyond yourself? You are the result of a long chain of survival and love, a living mosaic of generations past.

Think about your nose, your eyes, the shape of your face. These are not just random traits but the legacy of ancestors who faced unimaginable challenges to survive and thrive. That nose you might not like? It could be the same one that allowed your ancestors to breathe in harsh climates. Those eyes you find too small? They might have seen breathtaking landscapes and guided your forebears through unknown lands.

Every characteristic you carry is the result of countless choices, of people who looked at each other and found themselves beautiful enough to join together and create life. Isn't that a powerful thought?

Self-acceptance does not mean ignoring the desire for improvement or personal care. It means embracing your essence, recognizing that your uniqueness is your greatest gift to the world. It means honoring the journey that led to your existence, respecting the heritage you carry with you.

When you start to see yourself through this lens, something magical happens. Insecurities begin to dissolve, replaced by a sense of wonder and gratitude. You start treating your body not as an object to be perfected, but as a living temple of history and resilience.

This shift in perspective has the power to transform not only how you see yourself but also how you relate to others. When you fully accept yourself, you become more compassionate, more open, more capable of seeing and appreciating the unique beauty in every person you meet.

So, the next time you look in the mirror, try to see beyond the superficial imperfections. See the strength of your ancestors, the resilience of past generations, the beauty of your uniqueness. Because you are not just yourself: you are the culmination of a millennia-long love story.

Step 8 - Letting Go of What Doesn't Belong to Us

Life is a constant flow of people, experiences, and opportunities. Yet, how often do we find ourselves desperately clinging to situations or relationships that no longer serve us? True emotional detachment begins with the ability to recognize when it's time to let go.

Imagine holding a handful of sand. The tighter you squeeze, the more the sand slips through your fingers. Similarly, the more we try to hold on to what is no longer ours, the more we risk losing ourselves in the process.

Detachment does not mean indifference or coldness. On the contrary, it is an act of profound respect for the natural flow of life. It means accepting that people change, situations evolve, and that sometimes the most loving thing we can do is allow something or someone to go their own way.

This principle applies not only to relationships but also to our beliefs, goals, and even our identities. How often do we cling to an image of ourselves that no longer reflects who we truly are? Or to a dream that no longer excites us, simply because we fear change?

Letting go requires courage. It means facing the unknown, embracing uncertainty. But it is in this space of vulnerability that we often find our true strength.

Think of all the times you resisted change, only to later realize it was exactly what you needed. Maybe it was the end of a relationship that paved the way for deeper love. Or a professional failure that pushed you toward your true calling.

Detachment also teaches us to live more fully in the present. When we stop clinging to the past or obsessively projecting into the future, we discover the richness of the present moment.

It's not about abandoning everything lightly but about wisely discerning what truly nourishes and helps us grow from what holds us back. It is an invitation to trust the process of life, to believe that what is meant for us will find us if we make space for it.

Step 9 - The Power of Self-Confidence

Self-confidence is not just a character trait; it is a transformative force that can redefine every aspect of your life. Too often, we confuse confidence with arrogance or think that self-confidence means never having doubts. But true confidence is something much deeper and more nuanced.

Think of someone you admire for their confidence. It's probably not someone who never makes mistakes, but rather someone who faces challenges with grace and resilience. True self-confidence does not come from perfection but from self-acceptance and the ability to navigate uncertainty.

This confidence manifests in countless subtle ways: in how you move, speak, and interact with others. It's not about always being the center of attention but about feeling comfortable in your own skin, regardless of the circumstances.

Cultivating this confidence requires practice and patience. Start by recognizing your strengths and celebrating your successes, no matter how small they may seem. Every time you overcome a challenge or learn something new, you are building your reserve of confidence.

But true confidence is also forged through failure. Paradoxically, it is the ability to fail, get back up, and keep going that builds indestructible confidence. Every time you face a fear or recover from a mistake, you prove to yourself that you are stronger and more resilient than you thought.

Self-confidence radically changes the way we relate to others. When you are confident, you don't feel the need to compete or put others down to feel valid. Instead, you can genuinely celebrate others' successes, knowing that another person's worth does not diminish your own.

This inner security acts like a beacon in the storm of relationships. It naturally attracts positive people and opportunities into your life while allowing you to gracefully walk away from toxic situations or relationships.

Remember, self-confidence is not a destination but a continuous journey. There will be days when you feel invincible and others when doubts take over. The important thing is to keep nurturing this confidence, day by day, choice by choice.

And so, as you cultivate this inner strength, you may find that the real magic does not lie in controlling others or circumstances but in the freedom that comes from fully trusting yourself.

Step 10 - Embracing Feminine (or Masculine) Energy

The journey towards detachment and emotional security often culminates in a profound rediscovery of one's essential energy, whether feminine or masculine. This is not a matter of biological gender, but rather about reconnecting with the primordial forces that reside within each of us. For many, especially for women, embracing feminine energy can be a transformative revelation. Feminine energy is not weakness, as some might mistakenly think. It is the strength of flowing water, which can be gentle and nurturing, yet powerful enough to shape mountains over time. Think of the contrast between pushing and pulling. Masculine energy tends to push, force, conquer. Feminine energy, on the other hand, pulls, invites, creates space. It is not passivity, but a magnetic power that naturally attracts what it needs. Embracing this energy means letting go of the constant need to "do" and learning the art of "being." It means trusting the natural flow of life instead of constantly trying to control it. It is like dancing with the universe instead of fighting against it. For men, or for anyone who identifies more with masculine energy, the path might be different but equally powerful. It could mean reconnecting with one's inner strength, the ability to protect and guide, but in a way that does not overwhelm or dominate others. Regardless of gender, this process of reconnecting with one's essential energy leads to greater authenticity and more balanced relationships. It allows you to interact with the world from a place of inner fullness, rather than from a sense of lack or need. In practice, embracing this energy might mean:

Cultivating intuition and inner listening Practicing receptivity instead of constant action Honoring the natural cycles of the body and nature Expressing creativity in all its forms Nurturing oneself and others in deep and meaningful ways

As you integrate this energy into your life, you might notice subtle yet profound changes. Relationships become more fluid, opportunities seem to manifest more easily, and there is a general sense of harmony with the world around you. Remember, it is not about denying other parts of yourself, but about finding balance. It is an invitation to explore all facets of your being, to celebrate your complexity and uniqueness. And so, as you continue this journey of discovery and growth, let your essential energy, whether feminine or masculine, guide your path. In this authenticity, you will find not only the emotional detachment you seek, but also a deeper connection with yourself and the world around you.

Chapter 14:
3 Signs Of Healing

In this chapter, we won't focus on the detailed process of healing or the final achievement of emotional security. Instead, we'll explore those early indicators that show you're on the right path. Recognizing these signs can confirm that your efforts are indeed bearing fruit, even if the final goal still seems distant.

Every step in the healing journey, no matter how small, is a sign of progress. It's important to learn to see and appreciate these moments because they are what will guide you out of the darkness, towards greater awareness and emotional security. So, what are these signs? Let's proceed carefully and discover them together.

Sign 1: Responsibility in Relationships

Imagine being in a relationship where you constantly feel neglected and unappreciated. It's easy to think the problem lies entirely with the other person, but what if you started considering that you might have an active role in this dynamic? This is one of the first signs of healing from anxious attachment: the awareness of your own responsibility in choosing the types of relationships you engage in.

When living in an unhealed state of anxious attachment, it's common to feel like a victim of circumstances. You tend to think that it's always others who treat you poorly, who don't give you the love and attention you deserve. This sense of victimhood can become a self-perpetuating cycle, further fueling anxiety and insecurity. However, an important step towards healing is recognizing that you have the power to choose who you form relationships with and how these relationships develop.

Taking responsibility in relationships means acknowledging that, often, we are the ones pursuing emotionally unavailable people. This behavior can stem from attachment patterns formed during childhood when we sought the attention of emotionally distant parents or caregivers. This pattern repeats itself in adulthood, leading us to chase partners who cannot or will not provide the emotional security we need.

Becoming aware of this pattern is a sign that you are making progress on the path to healing. It means starting to make more conscious choices about the people you engage with. Instead of chasing those who cannot meet your emotional needs, you can choose to wait and seek out those who are capable of building an authentic and respectful connection.

Part of this process of taking responsibility also involves respecting others' boundaries. When we are anxious, we might tend to control or manipulate others to get the love and attention we desire. This can manifest in trying to change someone's mind about a relationship, ignoring their wishes and needs. Respecting others' boundaries means accepting their choices and autonomy, even if it means facing rejection or abandonment.

Awareness and respect for boundaries are crucial for building healthy and balanced relationships. It means recognizing that true love cannot be forced or manipulated but must come from mutual respect and a shared willingness to build a meaningful connection.

Acknowledging your responsibility in relationships is a painful but liberating process. It means taking control of your emotional destiny and starting to make choices that foster your own growth and well-being. It's a clear sign that you are beginning to heal from anxious attachment and building healthier and more fulfilling relationships.

Sign 2: Recognizing Unrealistic Fantasies

Have you ever had such an intense crush on someone that you imagined they were perfect in every way, even though you barely knew them? This phenomenon, known as limerence, is common among people with anxious attachment. It's a form of idealized infatuation where you attribute extraordinary qualities to the other person without any concrete evidence to back them up.

In the process of healing from anxious attachment, an important sign is the ability to recognize these unrealistic fantasies. Often, when in a state of limerence, you create an idealized image of the other person, ignoring any signals that don't fit this perfect vision. You tend to build an internal narrative where the other person embodies all the qualities you desire, even if the reality might be quite different.

Take, for example, the story of Emily. Emily met Jack at a party and was immediately struck by his charisma. She began to imagine Jack as the ideal partner: kind, caring, always available. However, as time went on, Emily realized that many of the qualities she attributed to Jack were products of her imagination. Jack wasn't as available or caring as she had thought, but Emily had ignored these signals to keep her fantasy alive.

Recognizing limerence is a crucial step towards healthier and more authentic relationships. When you start to see people for who they really are, rather than through the filter of your expectations and desires, you can build connections based on reality. This recognition can be painful, as it requires letting go of your fantasies and facing reality, but it is a clear sign of healing.

Unrealistic fantasies can have a negative impact on your relationships. They can lead to disappointment when the other person inevitably fails to meet the high expectations you've created in your mind. Additionally, they can prevent you from seeing warning signs in a relationship, as you tend to minimize or ignore problematic behaviors to keep the fantasy alive.

Accepting reality for what it is, rather than trying to mold it to fit your fantasies, is essential. It means acknowledging that no one is perfect and that everyone has flaws and limitations. This not only leads to more genuine relationships but also helps build a foundation of trust and mutual respect, which is essential for an authentic emotional connection.

Recognizing unrealistic fantasies is a powerful sign of progress in the healing journey from anxious attachment. It allows you to see people for who they truly are, avoiding the traps of limerence, and building relationships based on reality and mutual acceptance.

Sign 3: The Importance of Self-Regulation

Imagine a particularly stressful day at work. You come home exhausted, with your mind full of negative thoughts. The first thing you do is pick up the phone and call a friend, hoping that a conversation can calm and reassure you. This need to seek external validation and comfort is common among people with anxious attachment. However, healing involves the ability to find security and serenity within yourself, without always relying on others.

Emotional self-regulation is the ability to manage your emotions autonomously. For those with anxious attachment, this can seem like an insurmountable challenge. Often, the immediate response to a stressful situation is to seek someone who can provide comfort and reassurance. However, developing the ability to self-regulate means building a trusting relationship with yourself, learning to recognize and manage your emotions independently.

Have you ever tried to stop for a moment when you feel overwhelmed and ask yourself: "What am I feeling right now? Why do I feel this way?" Recognizing your emotions and accepting them without judgment is the first step to managing them effectively. This awareness process may seem difficult at first, but with practice, it becomes a valuable resource for emotional well-being.

One of the most effective strategies for developing self-regulation is the practice of mindfulness. Spend a few minutes each day meditating, focusing on your breath and allowing thoughts to flow without clinging to them. This practice helps develop greater awareness of the present moment, reducing anxiety and improving stress management.

Additionally, keeping an emotion journal can be helpful, where you write down your feelings and reflect on them. This allows you to identify emotional patterns and find more effective ways to cope. Physical activity, such as yoga or running, is another powerful tool for releasing tension and improving mood. Even engaging in creative hobbies, like drawing or music, can be an effective way to express and regulate your emotions.

Remember that self-regulation doesn't mean isolating yourself from others or avoiding asking for help. Rather, it means developing a solid emotional foundation that you can rely on, reducing dependence on others for your emotional well-being. Building this capability takes time and practice, but the benefits are immense: more balanced relationships, greater self-esteem, and a sense of emotional autonomy that can transform the quality of your life.

Your Opinion Matters

"Helping one person might not change the whole world, but it could change the world for one person." — Unknown

People who help others expecting nothing in return experience a greater sense of fulfillment and lead a more rewarding life. I'd like to create the opportunity to deliver this value to you during your reading experience.

I have a simple question for you: Would you help someone you've never met if it didn't cost you anything and you didn't receive any credit for it?

If so, I have an ask to make on behalf of someone you do not know. And likely never will. They are just like you, or like you were a few years ago: eager to understand their attachment style better, full of desire to improve their relationships, seeking information but unsure where to find it... this is where you come in.

The only way for me to achieve my goal of helping people build secure relationships is first by reaching them. And most people do judge a book by its cover (and its reviews). If you have found this book valuable so far, would you please take a brief moment now and leave an honest review of the book and its contents? It will cost you nothing and take less than 60 seconds.

I appreciate all reviews, whether positive or negative, and I will read them personally. Your review helps:

- One more person understand their attachment style

- One more soul begin the process of building secure relationships

- One more life change for the better

To make that happen... takes less than 60 seconds... and is super simple to do...

Scan to leave a review on
Amazon if you live in the US

Scan to leave a review on
Amazon if you live in the UK

Scan to leave a review on
Amazon if you live in Canada

Scan to leave a review on
Amazon if you live in Australia

Thank you from the bottom of my heart.

Conclusion

Throughout the pages of this book, we've embarked on a deep and transformative journey. We began by exploring the origins of anxious attachment, understanding how past experiences and relational patterns can influence our present. We then delved into practical strategies to recognize and address anxiety symptoms in relationships, utilizing techniques of self-reflection, communication, and trust-building. Most importantly, we've learned that change is possible and that every step toward emotional security is a significant achievement.

One crucial aspect to remember is that the path to secure attachment is not linear. There will be days when you feel you've made tremendous progress and others when old anxieties seem to resurface. This is normal. Personal growth is a process that requires time, patience, and a generous dose of self-compassion. There is no perfect path, but every step forward, no matter how small, contributes to building a more solid foundation for your future relationships.

A key point in our journey has been the importance of self-awareness. We've discussed how recognizing your behavior patterns and emotional reactions is the first step to changing them. This awareness allows you to break the cycle of anxiety and choose healthier and more secure responses. Cultivating a practice of self-reflection, perhaps through meditation or journaling, can be a powerful ally in this process. Knowing yourself gives you the power to rewrite your relational story.

We've also explored the crucial role of communication in relationships. Being able to express your needs and desires clearly and respectfully is fundamental to building authentic and reciprocal connections. This means not only speaking but also actively listening to your partner, striving to understand their emotions and perspectives. Effective communication is a two-way street that requires openness, vulnerability, and mutual respect.

In the context of intimate relationships, building trust is another fundamental pillar. Trust is not something that is obtained once and for all, but is a continuous construction nourished by small daily gestures. Being reliable, keeping promises, and showing empathy are all concrete ways to strengthen mutual trust. However, remember that self-trust is also essential. Feeling confident in yourself and your relational abilities will allow you to enter relationships with a more solid foundation.

Another essential lesson has been the importance of external support. You don't have to face this journey alone. Whether it's a therapist, a support group, or trusted friends, having someone to share your experiences and challenges with can make a significant difference. External support not only provides comfort but also offers new perspectives and tools to address difficulties.

Finally, I want to emphasize the importance of celebrating your progress. Every small step toward a more secure attachment deserves to be acknowledged and celebrated. These progressions are a testament to your commitment and willingness to improve yourself and your relationships. The path may not always be easy, but every effort you make is an investment in your well-being and the quality of your future relationships.

Now that you've learned strategies to transform your anxious attachment into a secure attachment, I encourage you to put them into practice in your daily life. Embrace the journey with patience and kindness towards yourself. Each step forward brings you closer to more authentic and fulfilling relationships. Be proud of your path and continue to cultivate self-awareness and personal growth.

On a personal note, the journey towards emotional and relational security is unique to each of us, but your determination to improve is already an extraordinary achievement. I wish you to find inner peace and joy in your relationships, may they be full of love, understanding, and mutual respect.

Good luck on your journey! May you find the happiness and connection you seek.

About the Author

Susan Collins is a dedicated author and mentor focused on anxious attachment recovery and helping readers build secure, intimate relationships. For many years, Susan has explored and practiced emotional healing techniques, concentrating on overcoming anxious attachment through a journey of personal growth and self-awareness.

Susan's journey toward understanding anxious attachment began with her own personal experiences. Growing up in a family environment characterized by unstable relationships, she developed anxious attachment early on. This led her to experience many difficulties in her adult relationships, often feeling insecure and in need of constant reassurance.

After facing numerous relational challenges, Susan decided to take control of her life and address her attachment style. She embarked on an intensive path of research and practice, discovering the importance of developing a secure attachment style. She attended workshops, underwent therapy, and studied attachment psychology in depth. This journey led her to a deeper understanding of herself and relational dynamics, allowing her to live more authentically and harmoniously with others.

Susan has found great fulfillment in transforming her attachment style, uncovering greater creativity and the ability to live in alignment with her true self. Having experienced the transformative benefits of living with greater inner peace and wisdom, she became passionate about sharing this opportunity for growth with others.

Susan continues to dedicate time to daily meditation and practices yoga, finding joy and serenity in her routines. In her free time, she enjoys spending moments in nature, exploring new places with her two dogs, and engaging in creative activities that enrich her life.

www.ingramcontent.com/pod-product-compliance
Lightning Source LLC
Chambersburg PA
CBHW072252270326
41930CB00010B/2361